Art Deco Fashion Coloring Book

30 Coloring Pages for Adults of George Barbier Illustrations

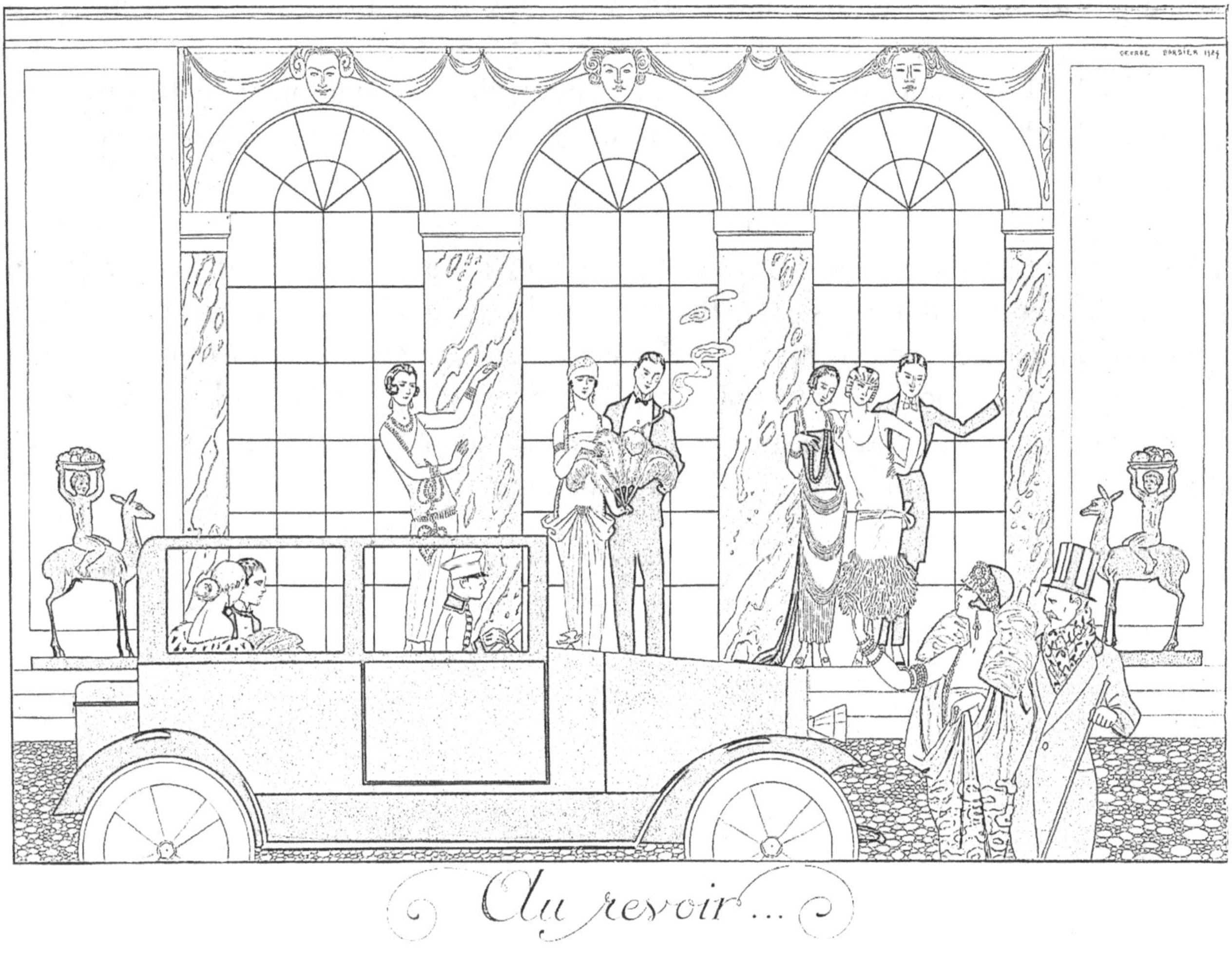

Au revoir...

Ada Ashley

In this art coloring book, you will find 30 most beautiful art deco illustrations from a famous illustrator of the period, George Barbier, reproduced true to original in light grayscale, perfect for realistic coloring and art therapy relaxation. Illustrations are reproduced without hard outlines for the opportunity to color them as actual artwork and be proud to cut out and display. In addition to coloring, this book allows you to practice drawing, shading, and tracing based on the artwork of a master illustrator. Color plates are included on the covers for reference.

The advantage of grayscale coloring over regular coloring is that the shading is already done, providing the depth and dimension to the final result. It also allows you to use the existing shadows for guidance. The general rule for grayscale coloring is simply to apply light colors over light gray areas, medium colors over medium gray areas, and dark colors over dark gray areas. Alternatively, you can start lightly with one color over larger areas and gradually add darker layers on top of it if you want more shading.

Ada Ashley

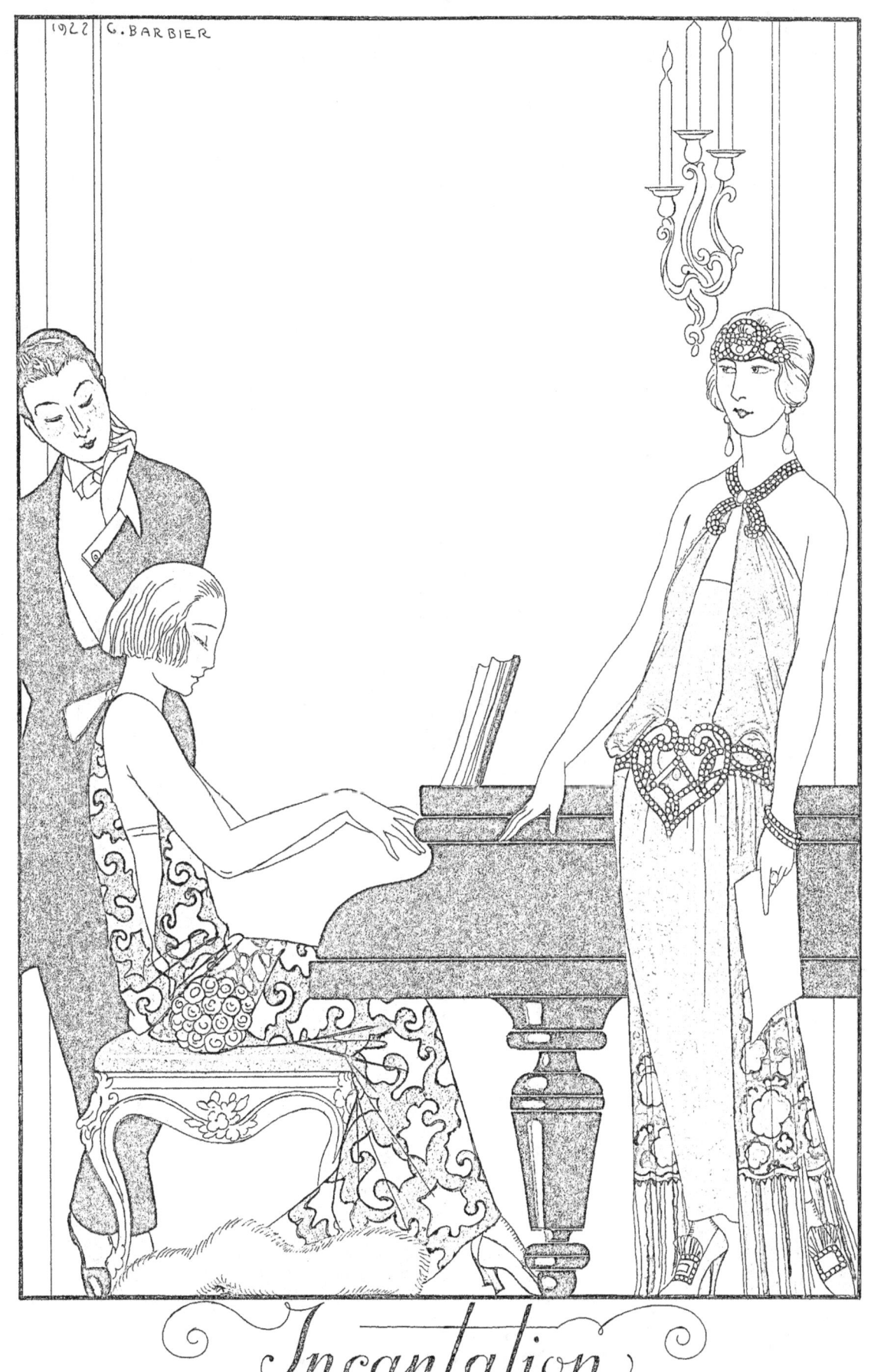

1922 G. BARBIER

Incantation

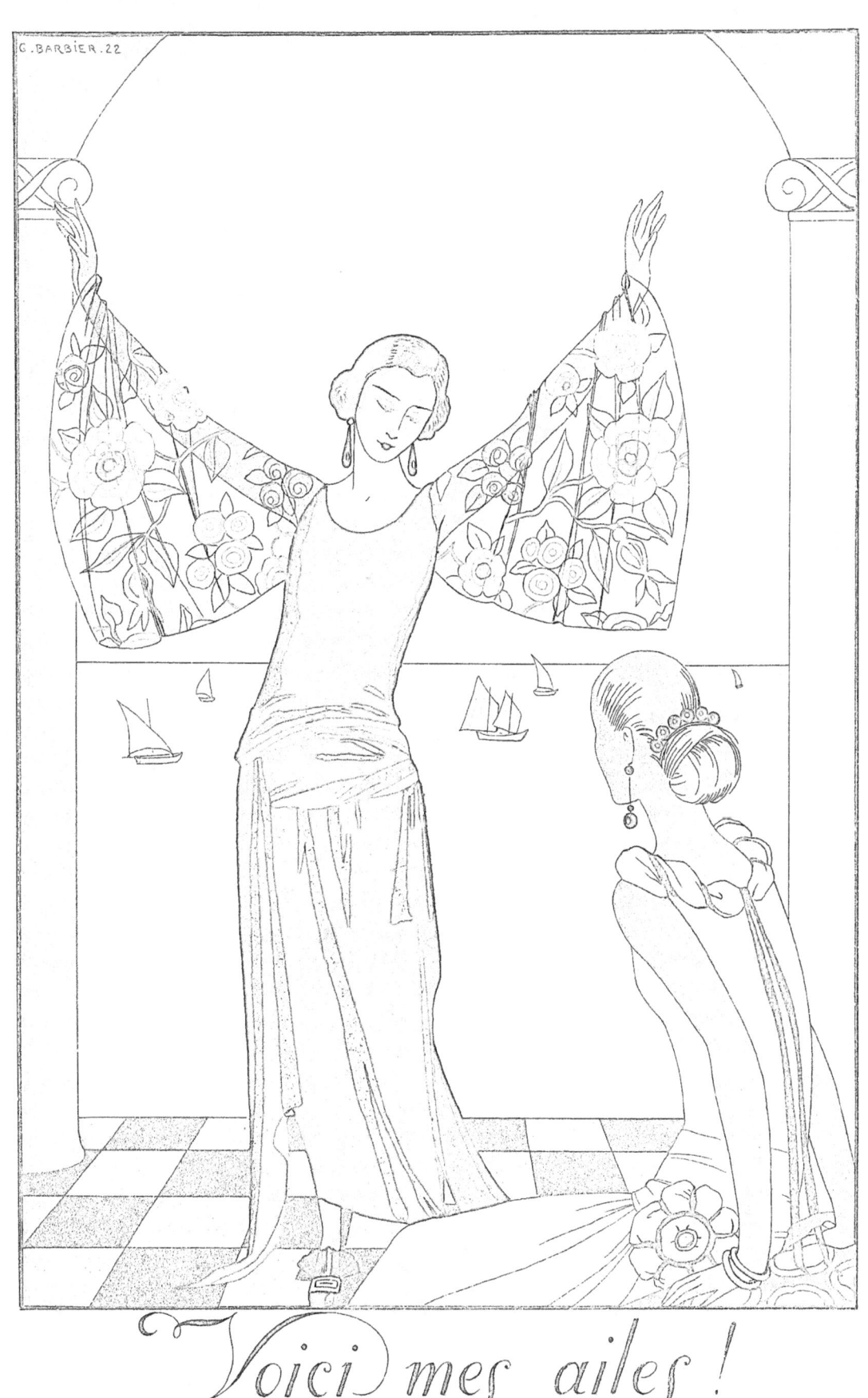

Voici mes ailes !

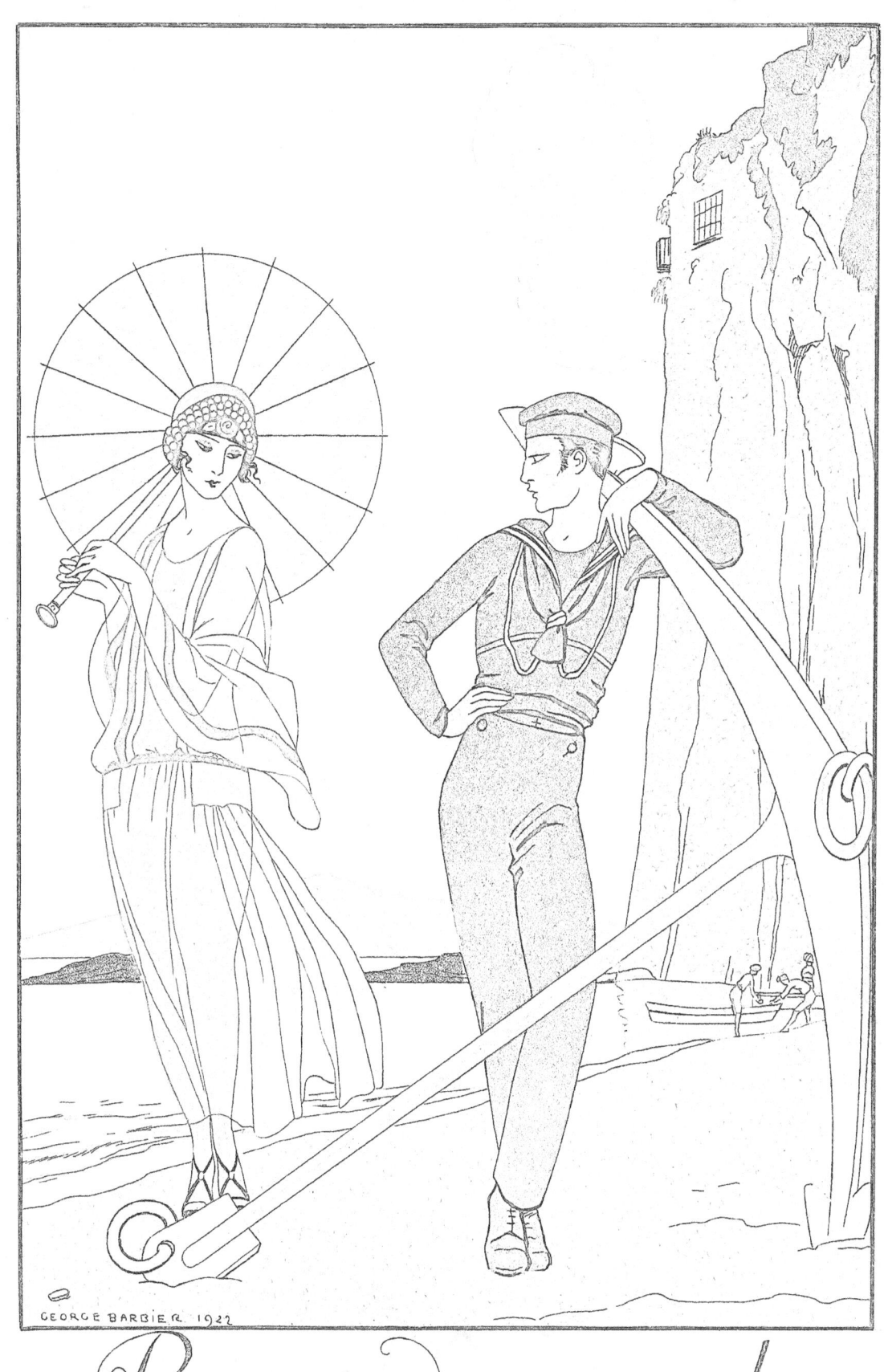

GEORGE BARBIER. 1922

Romance sans paroles.

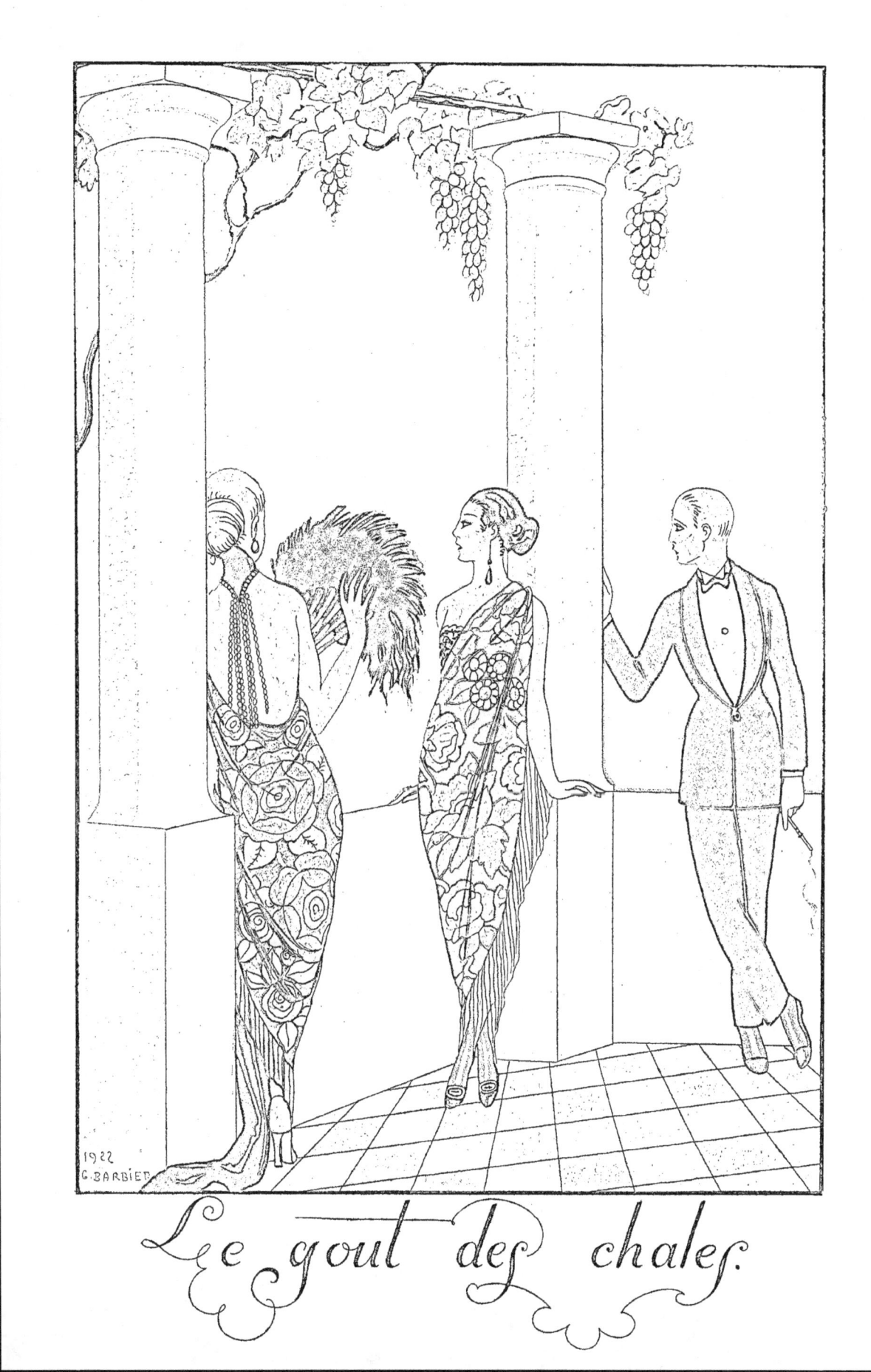

Le goût des châles.

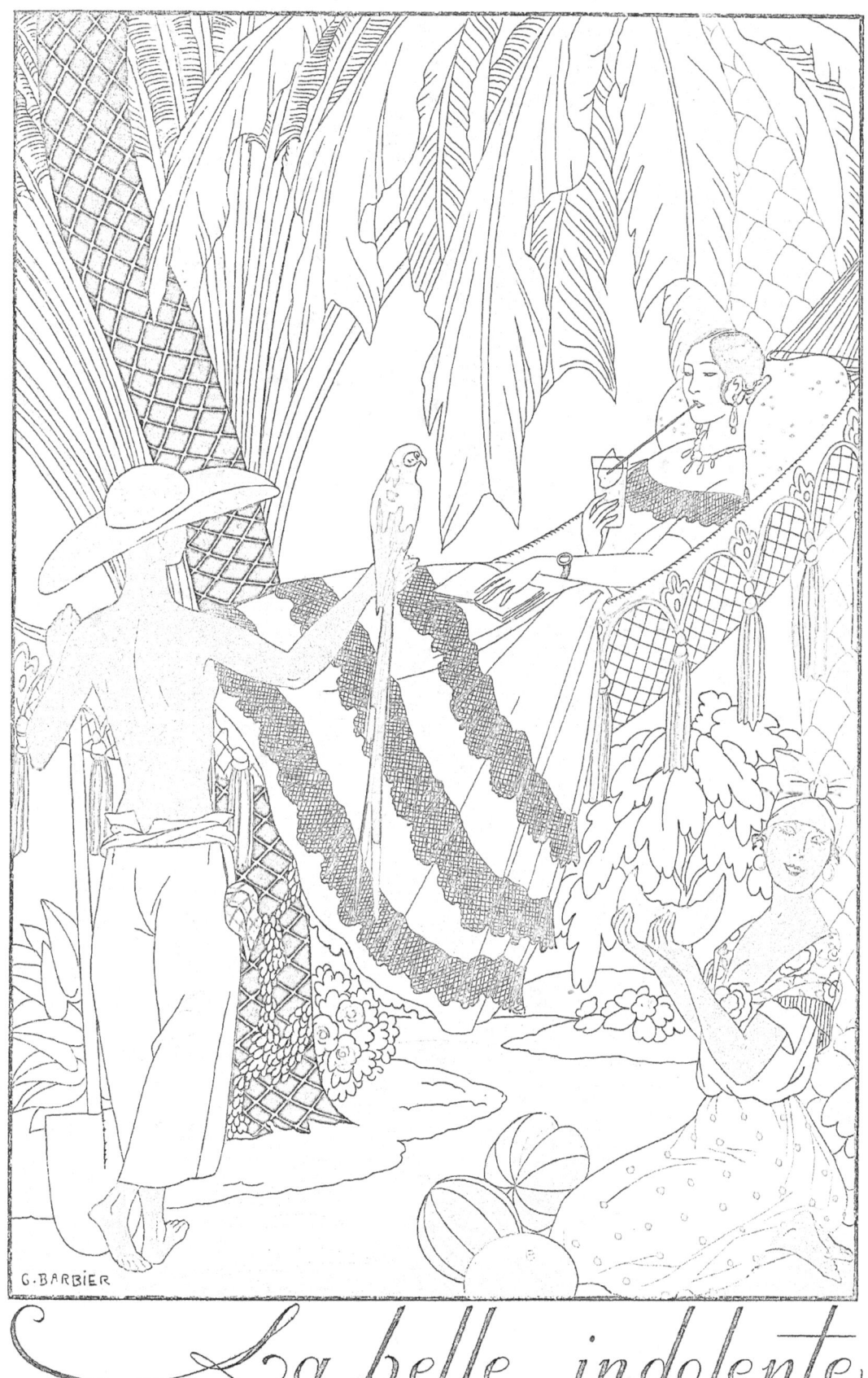

G. BARBIER

La belle indolente

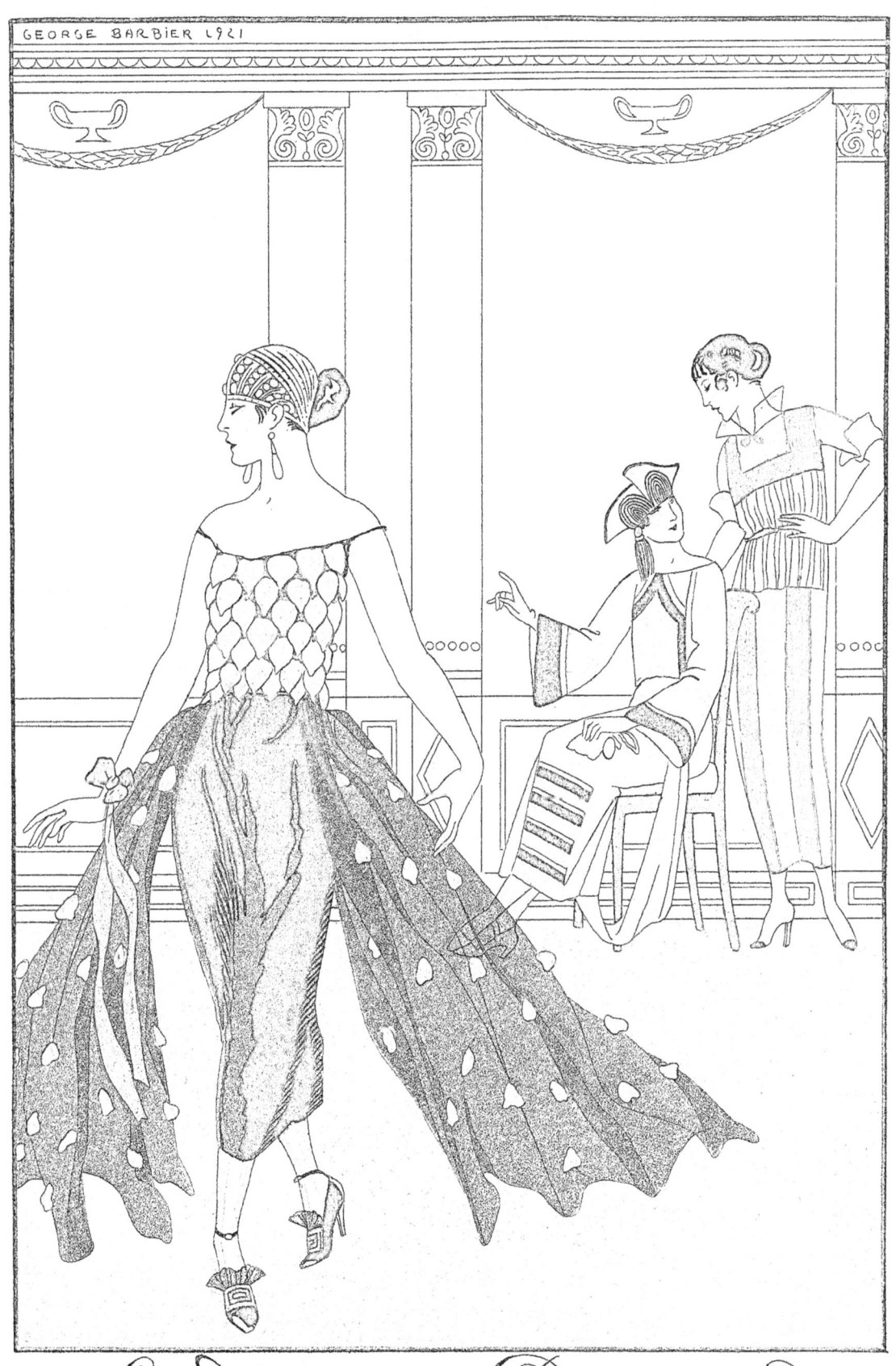

La Toilette Délicieuse.

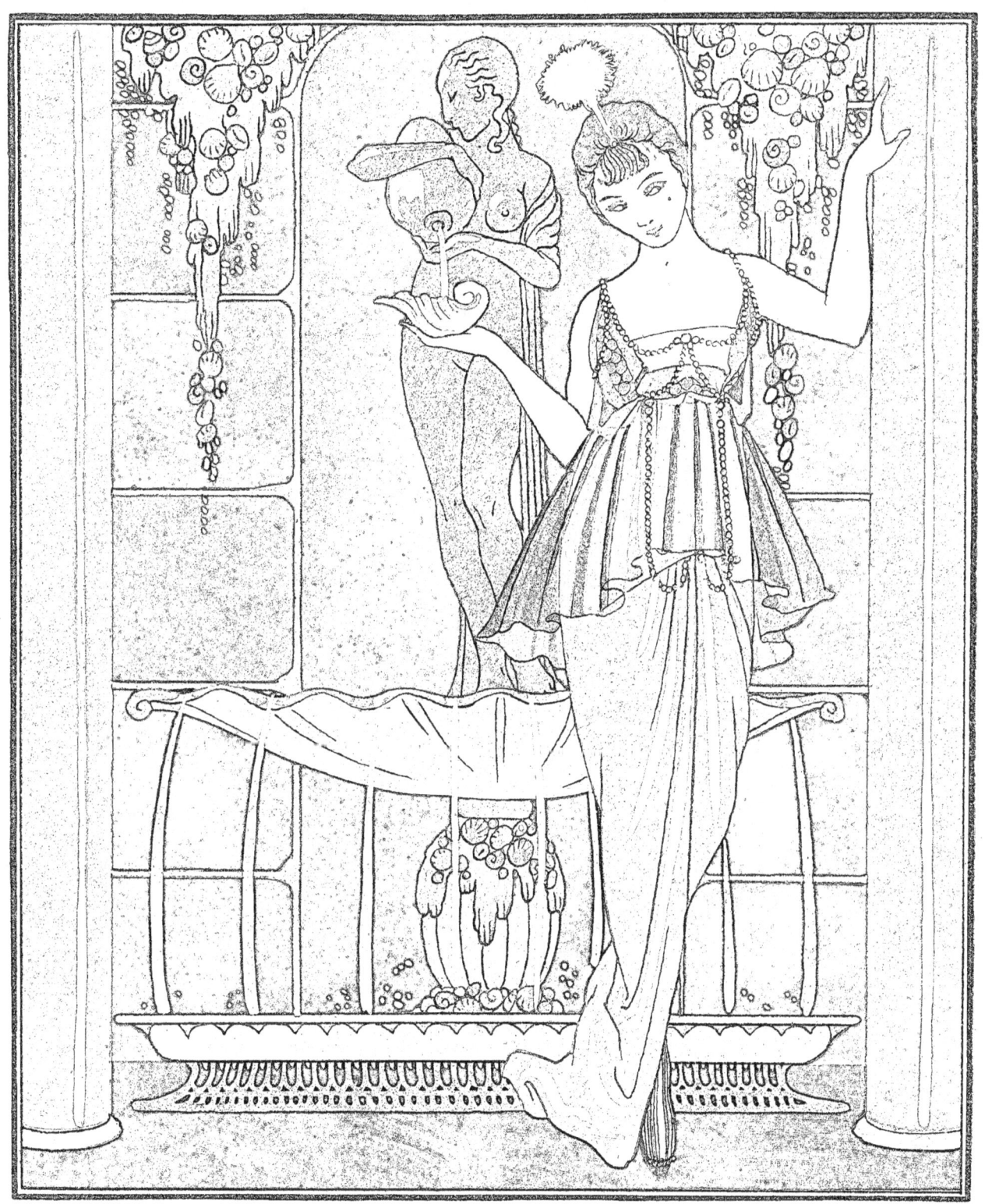

LA FONTAINE DE COQUILLAGES

Robe du soir de Paquin

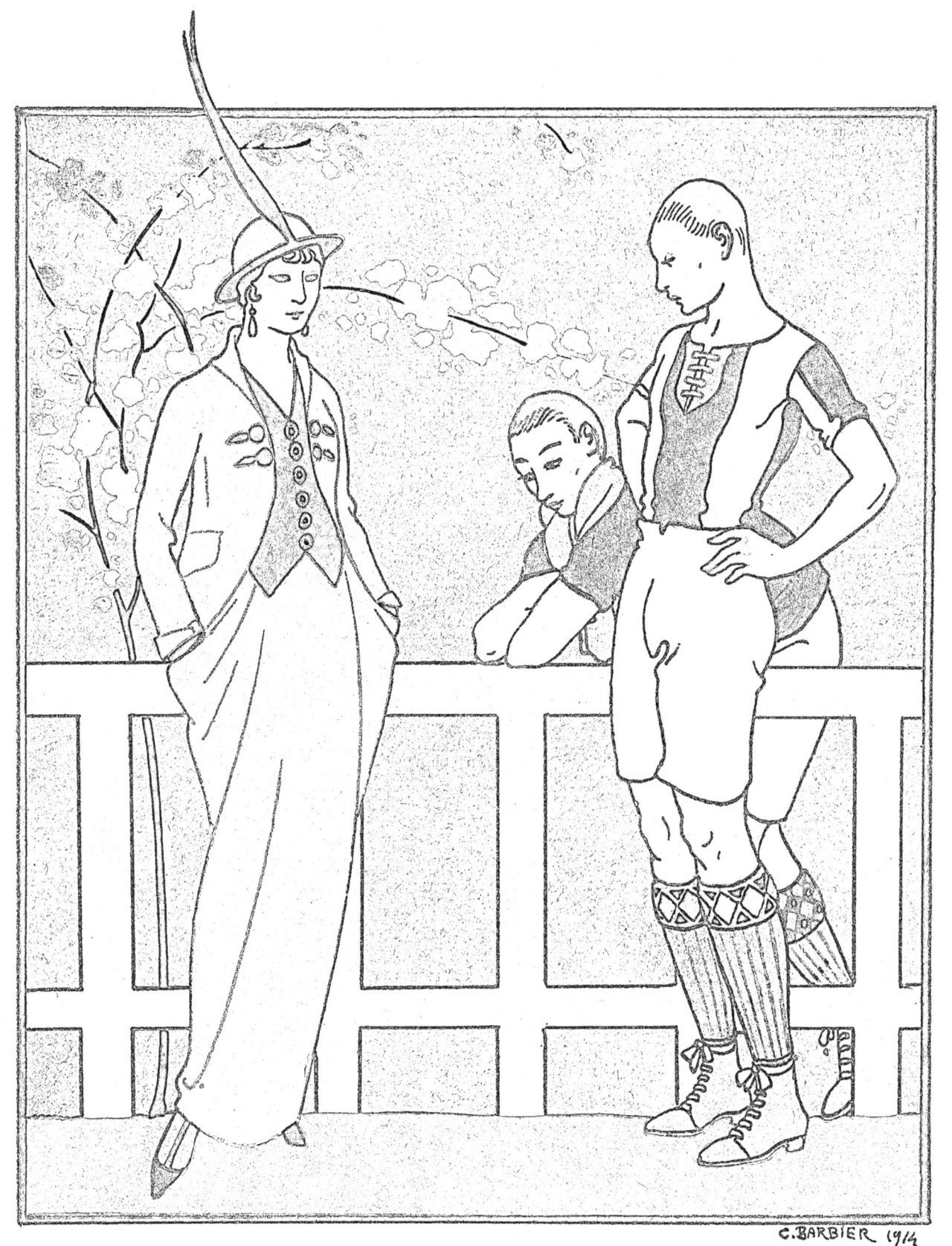

RUGBY
Costume tailleur de Redfern

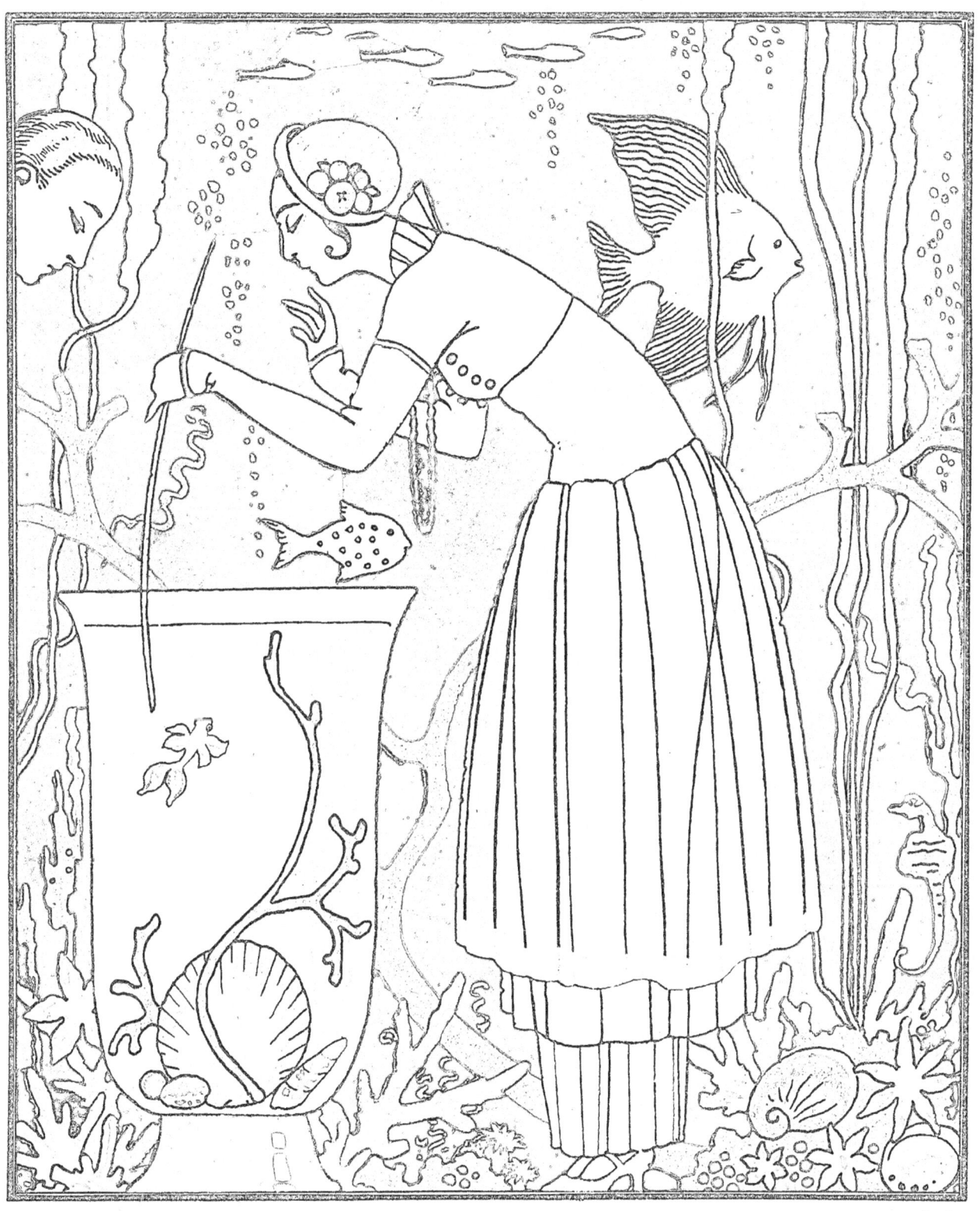

L'ÉTOURDISSANT PETIT POISSON...

Robe d'été

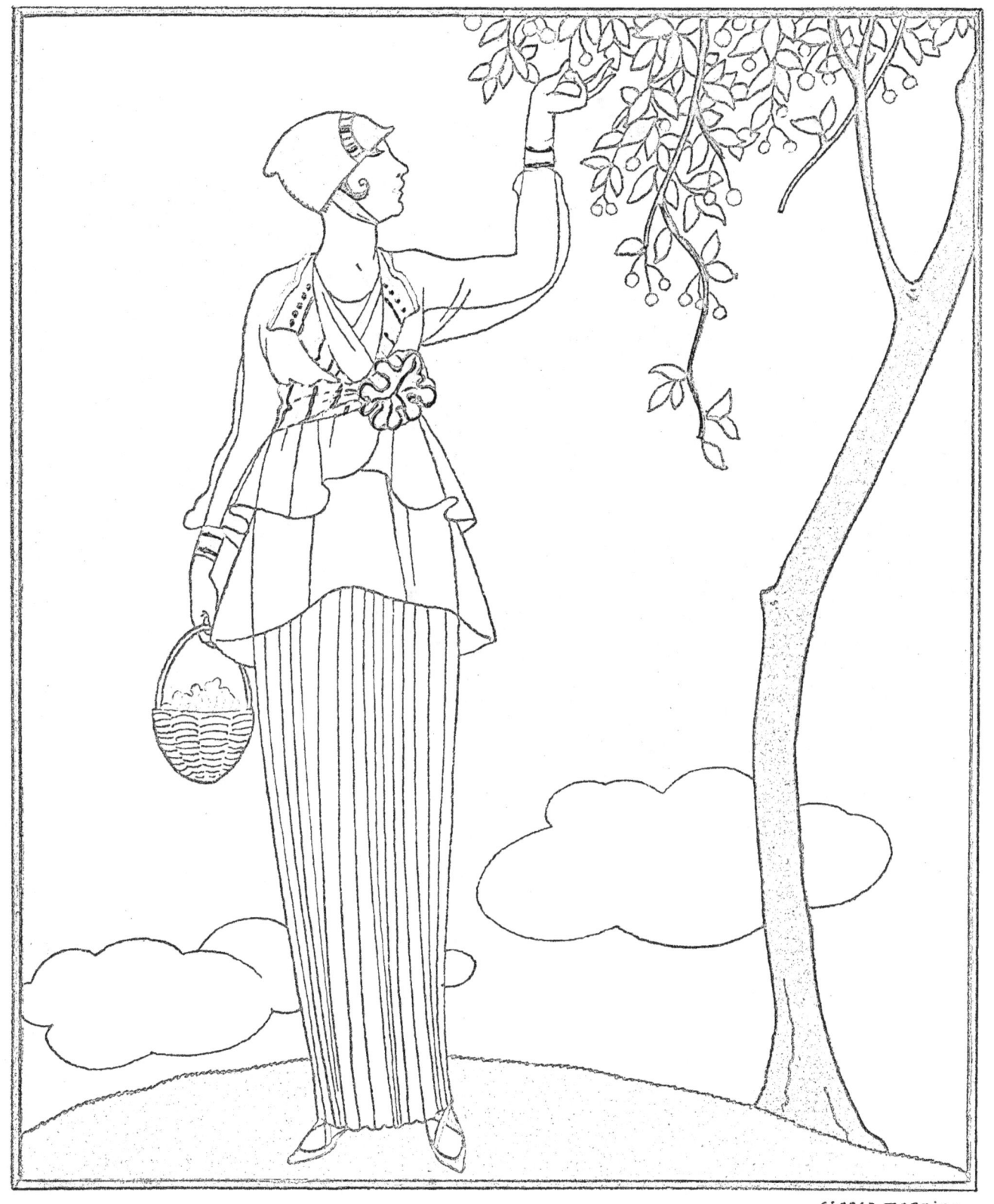

LA SAISON DES PRUNES MIRABELLES

Robe d'après-midi de Redfern

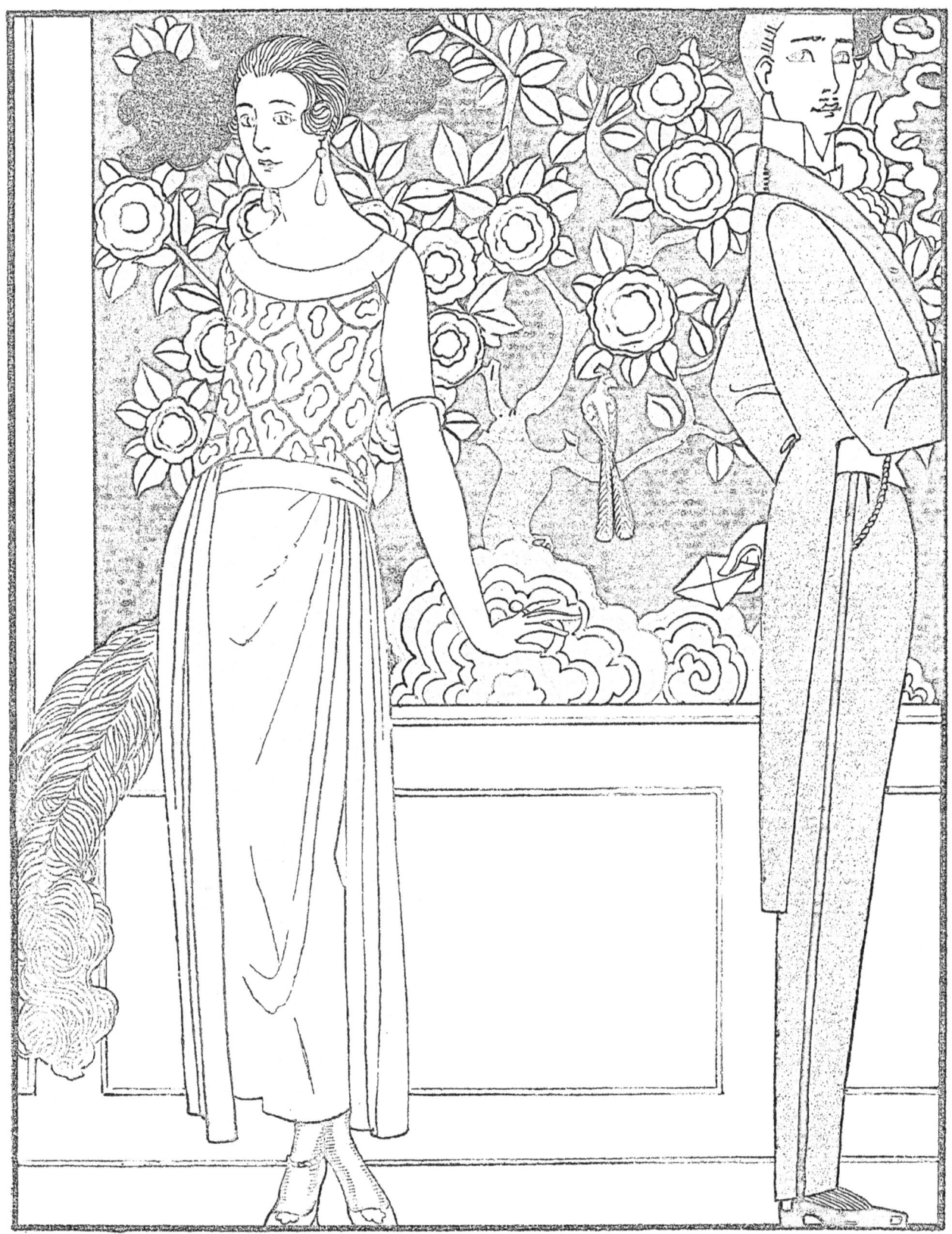

GEORGE BARBIER 1920

LA PREMIERE IMPRUDENCE

ROBE DU SOIR, DE BEER

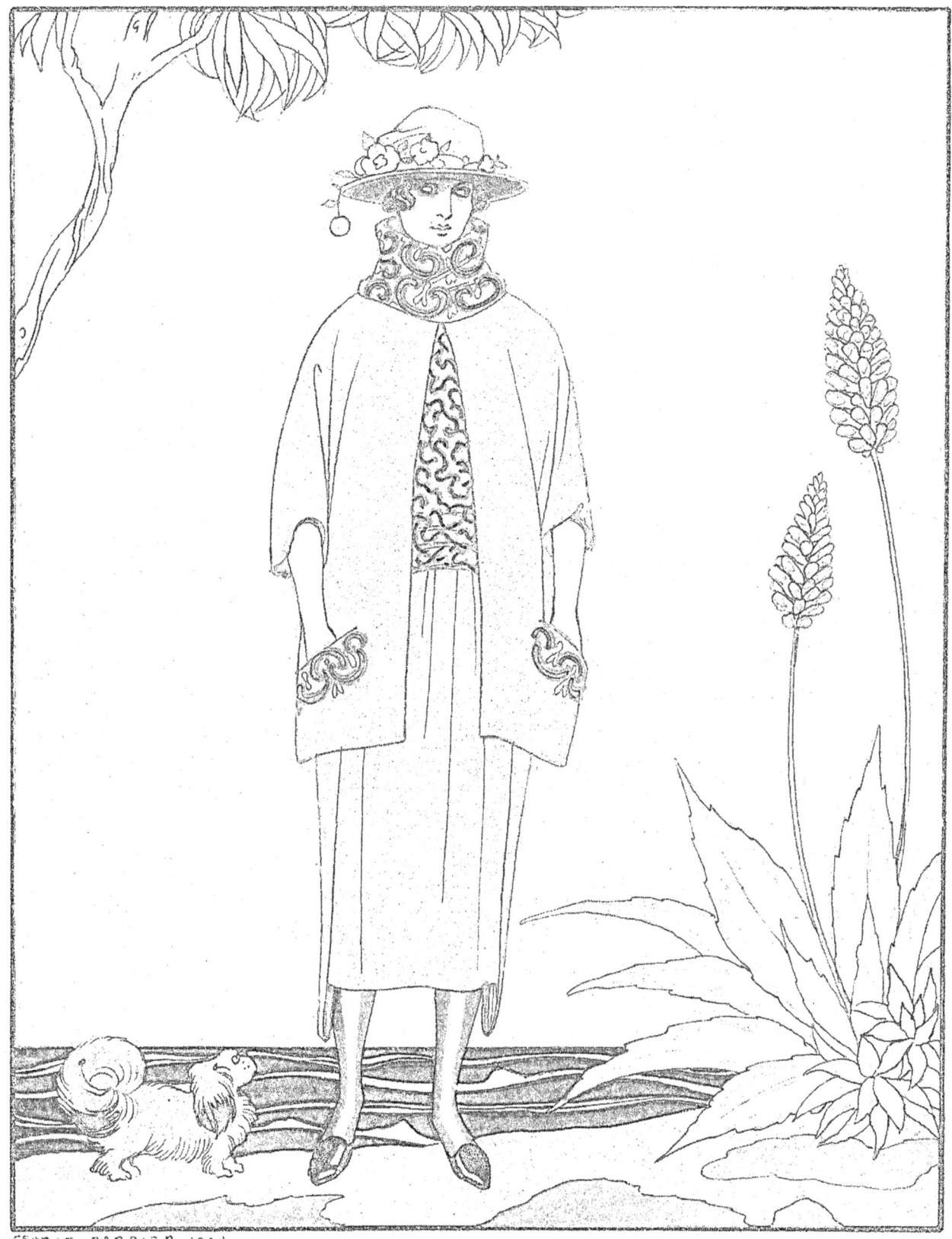

A PALM BEACH

TAILLEUR, DE WORTH

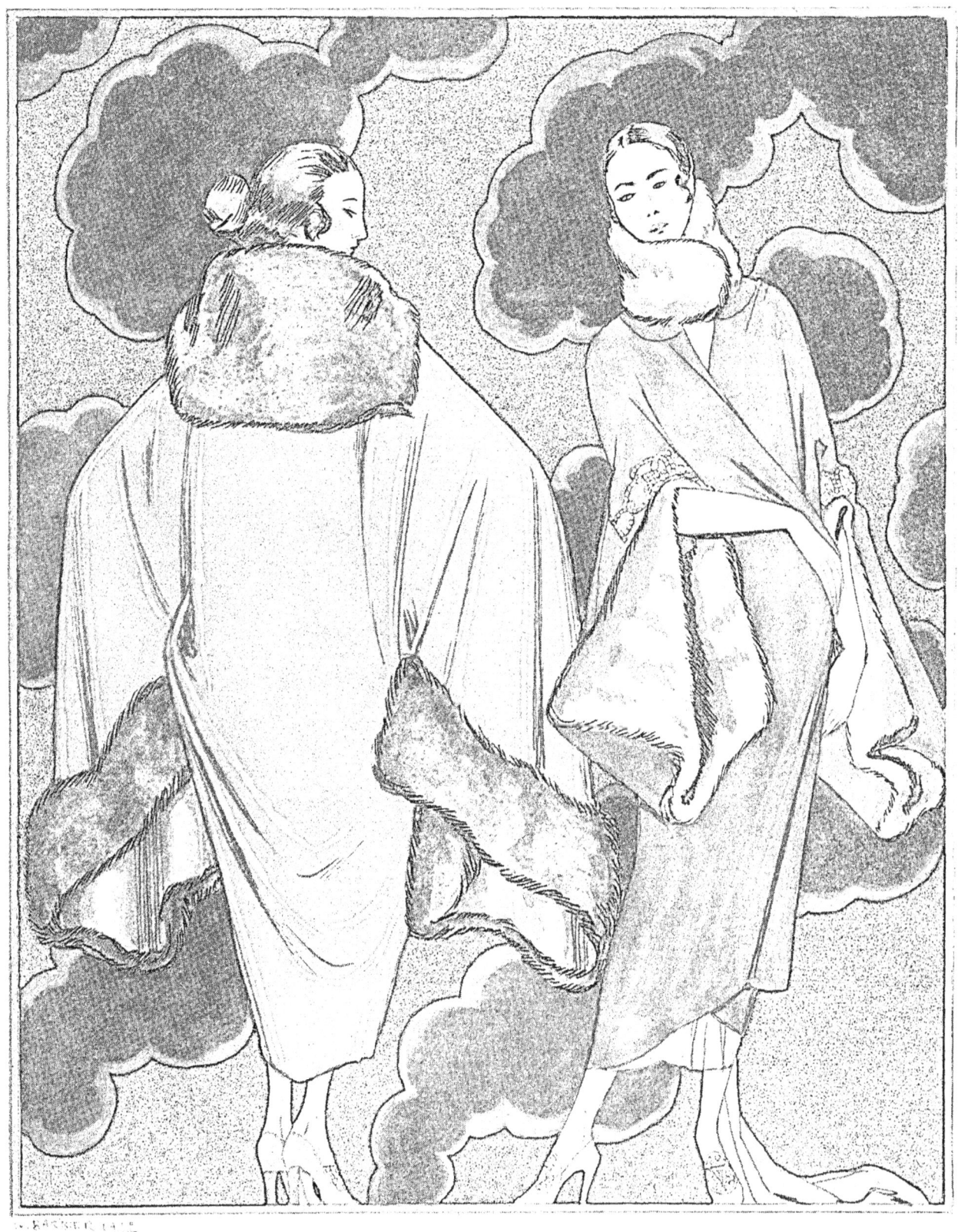

DEUX HEURES DU MATIN

MANTEAUX, DE WORTH

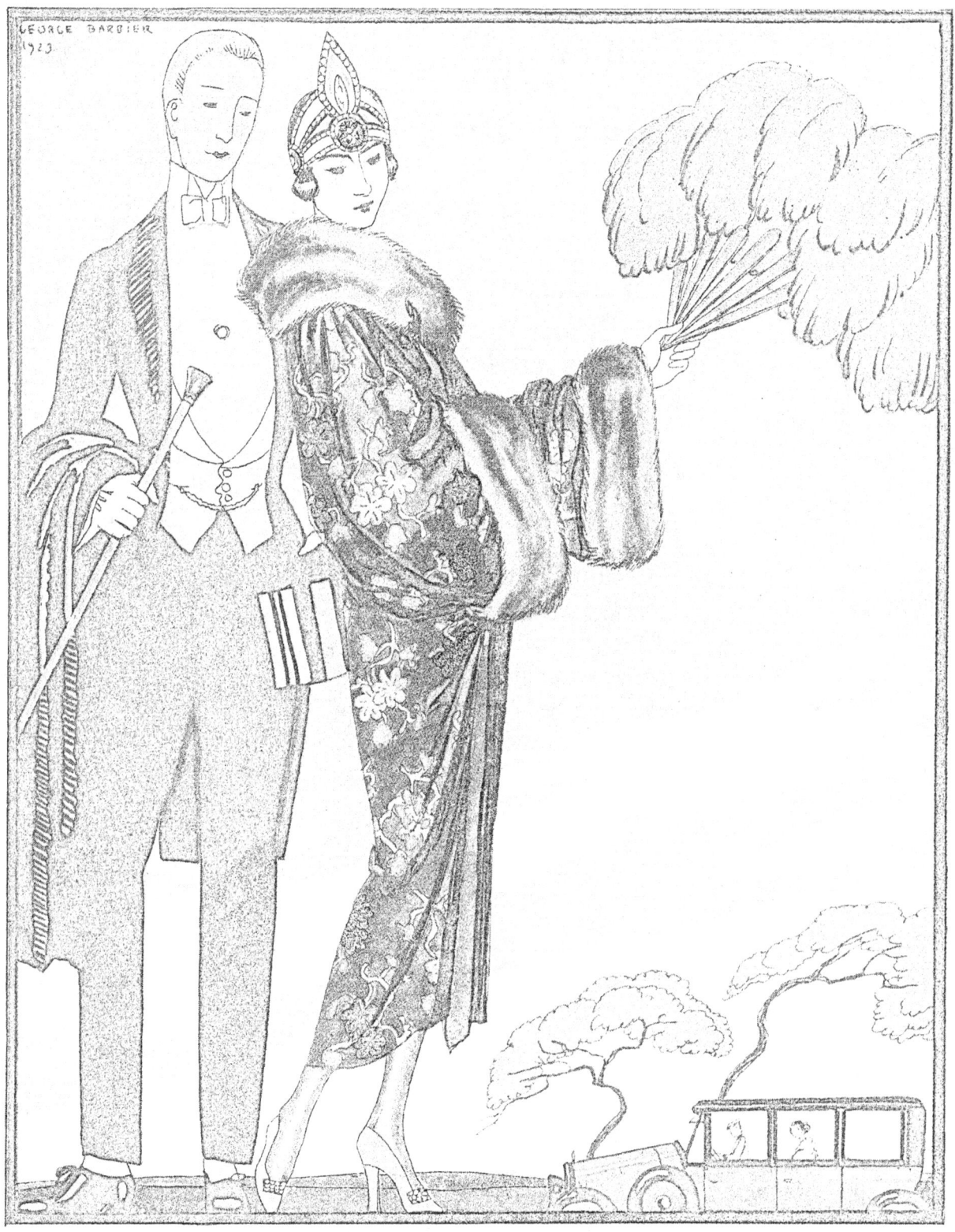

LE DÉPART POUR LE CASINO

MANTEAU DU SOIR, DE WORTH

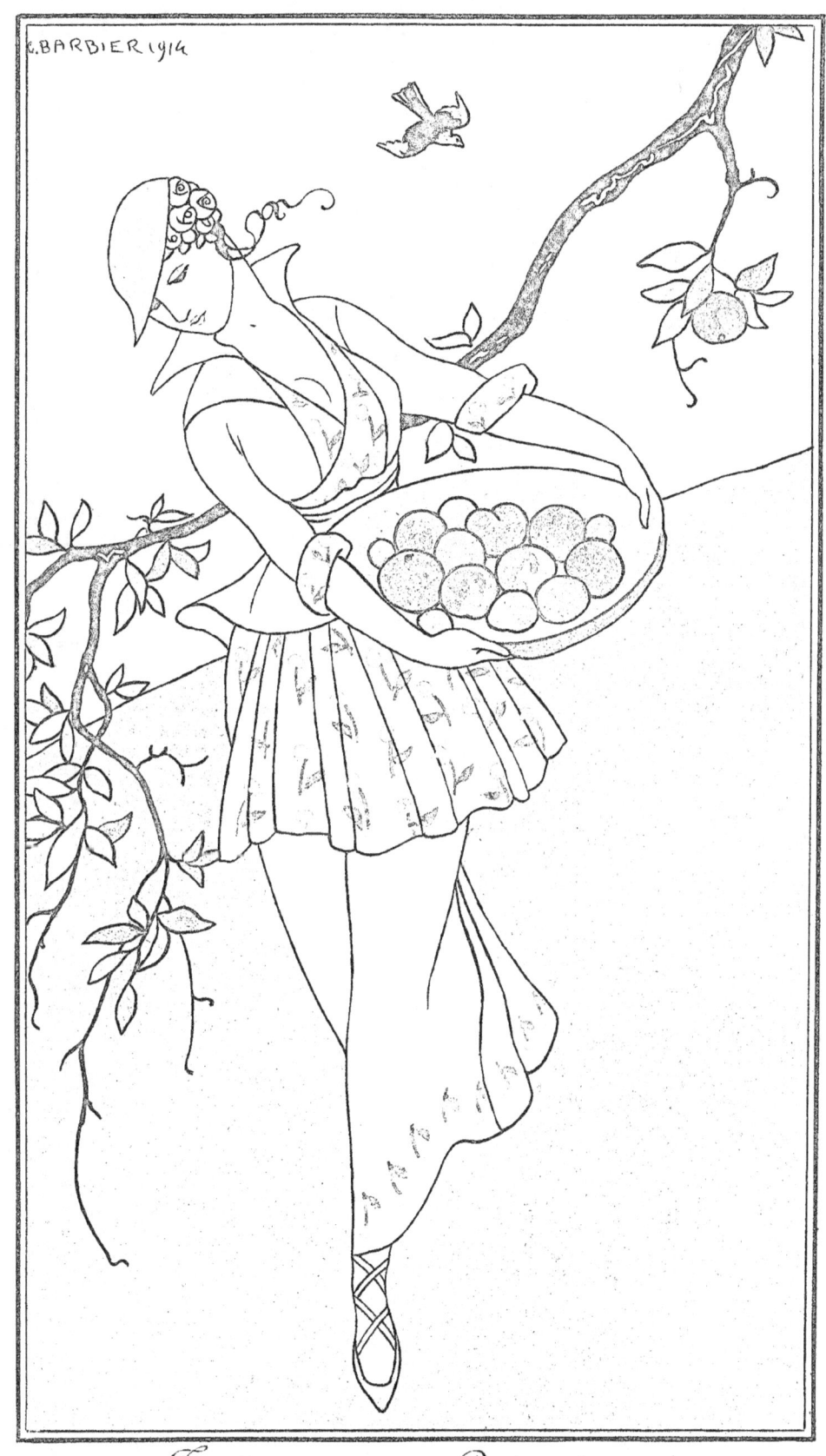

Toilette de taffetas imprimé
Chapeau de paille.

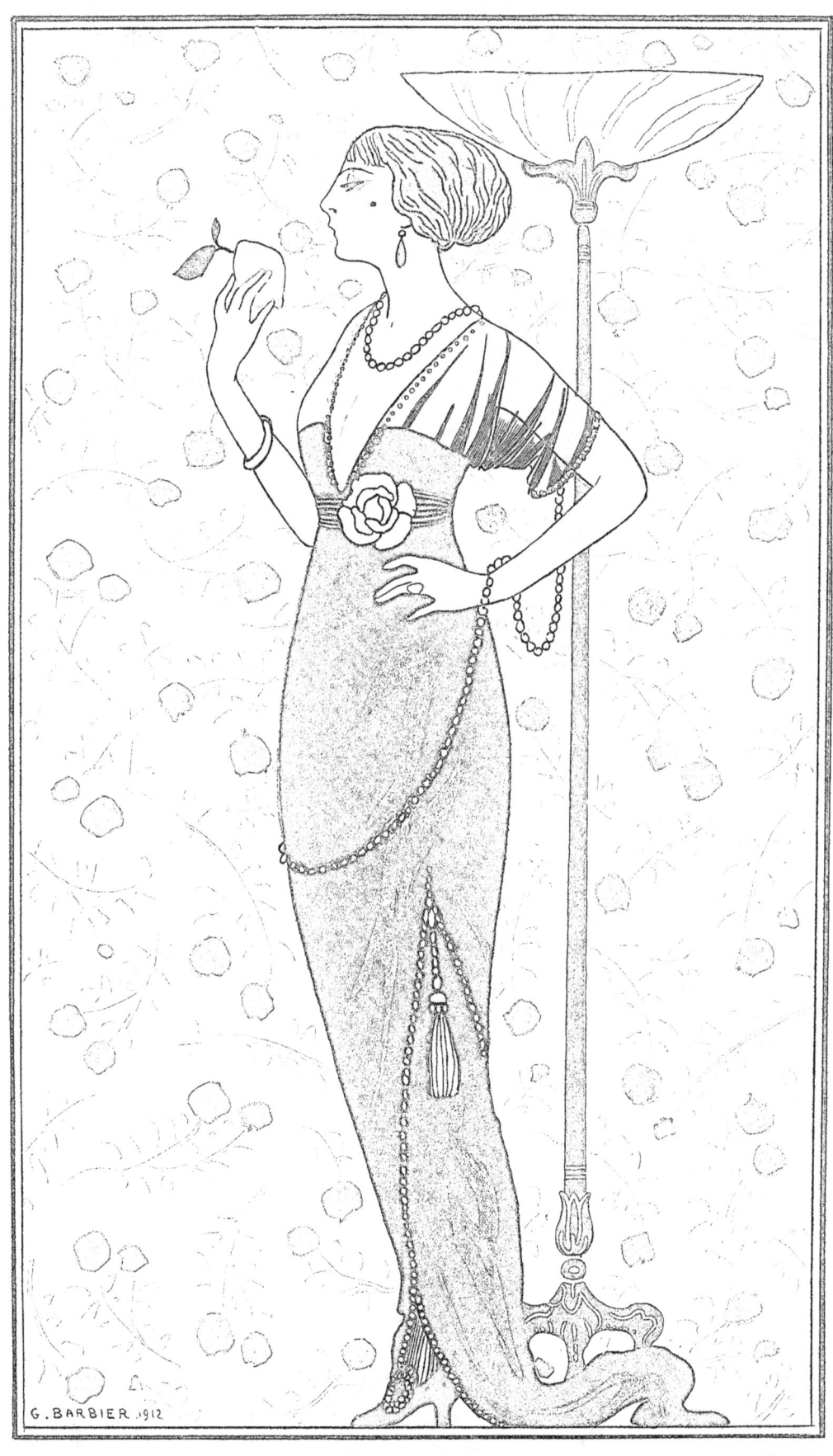

Robe du soir satin noir et tulle, bordée de brillants

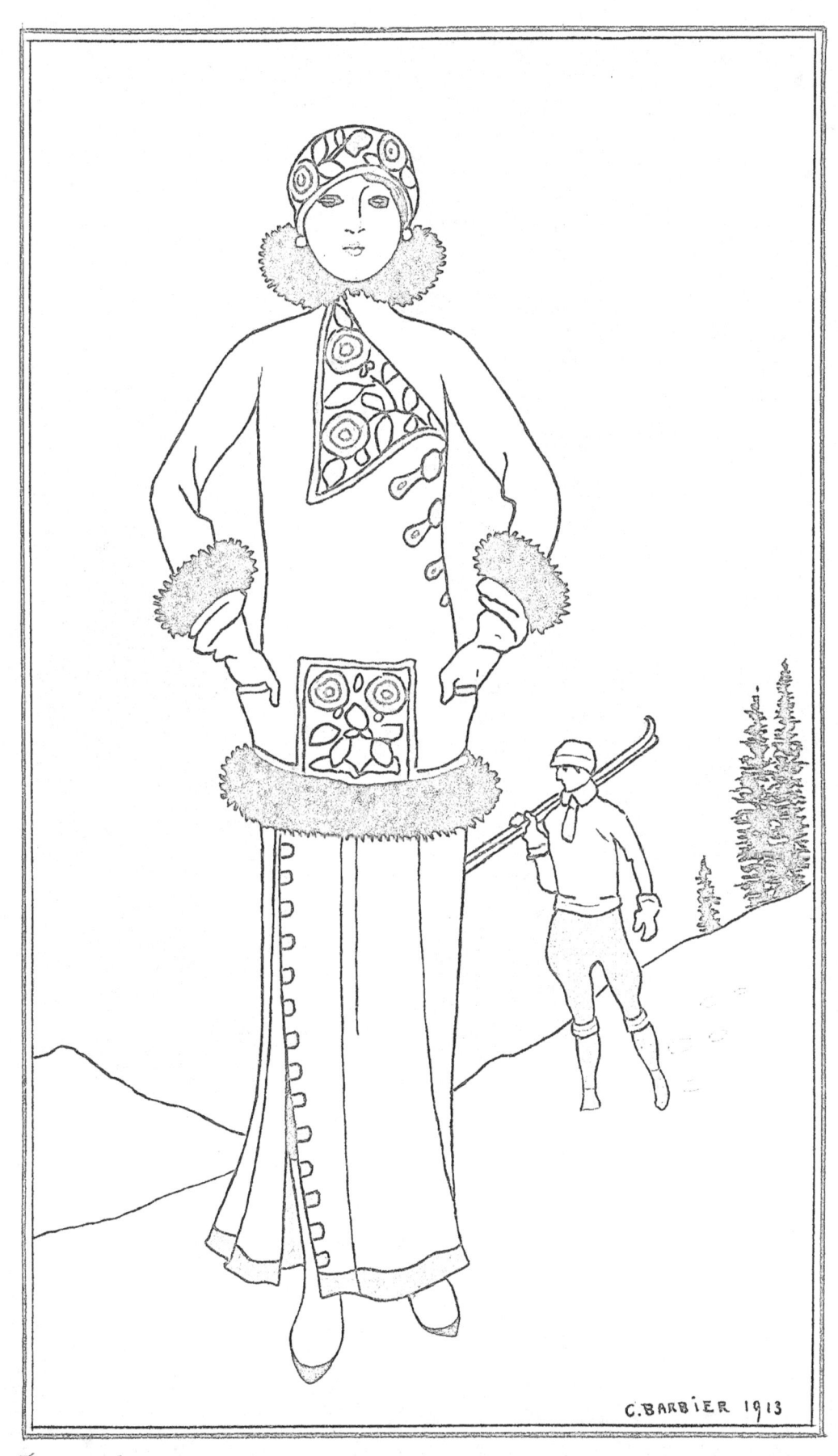

C.BARBIER 1913

Pour St. Moritz. Ratine blanche garnie de Skunks et brodée de Laines.

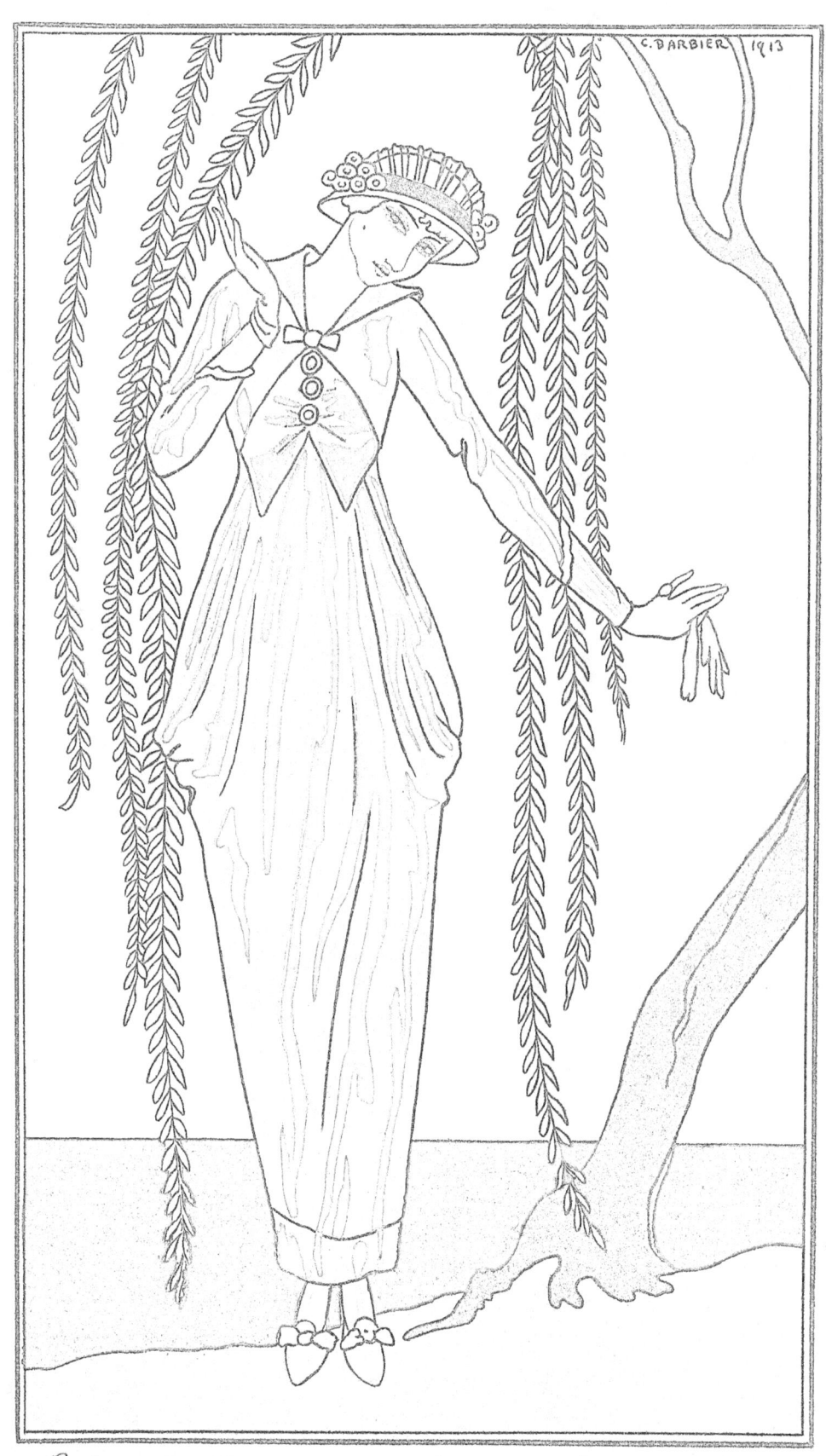

*Robe de taffetas gris à col et manchettes de linon,
et gilet de satin à boutons d'émail.*

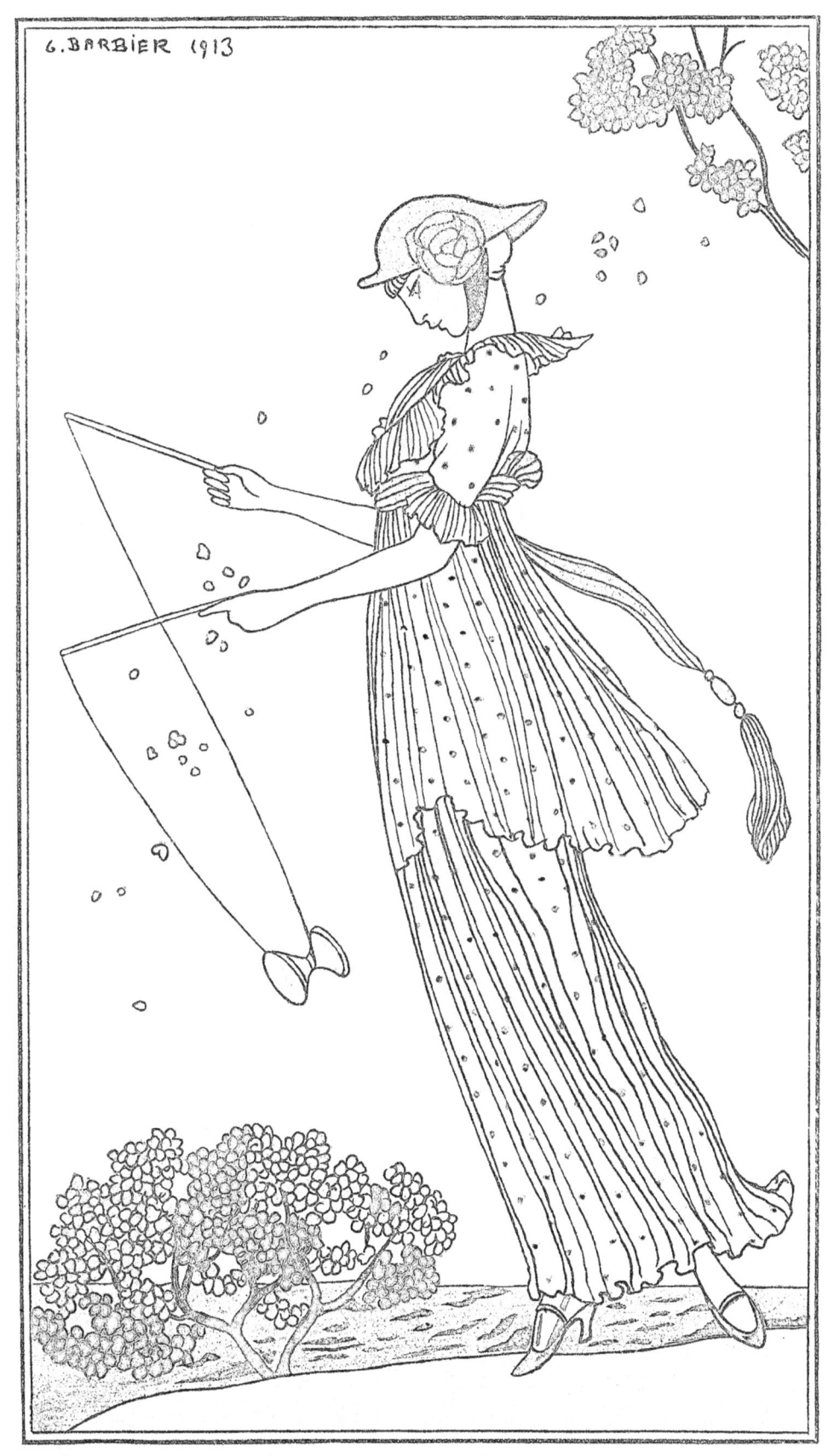

Robe de linon imprimé

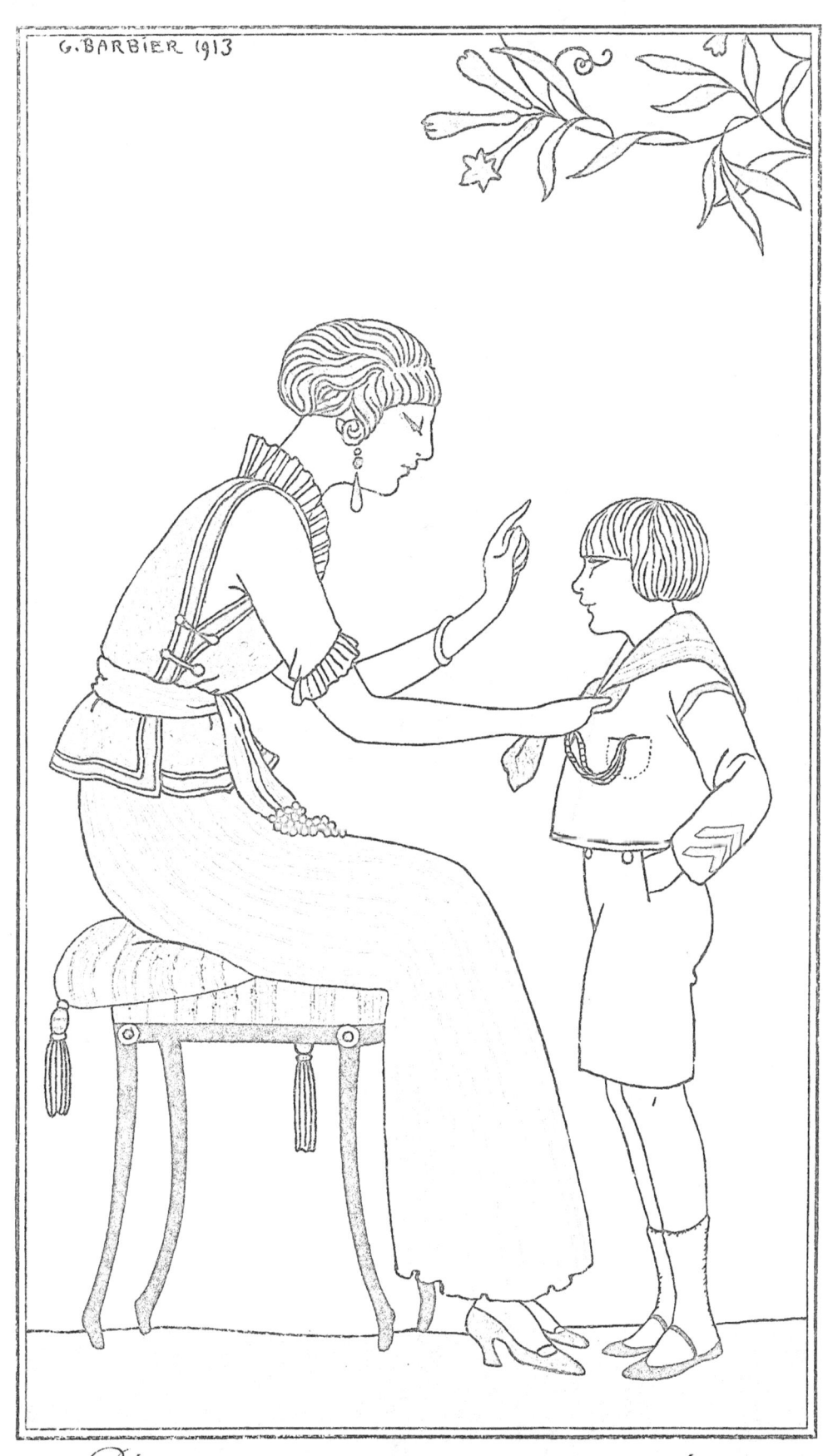

G. BARBIER 1913

Blouse japonaise en soie sur une jupe plissée.
Marin de toile blanche

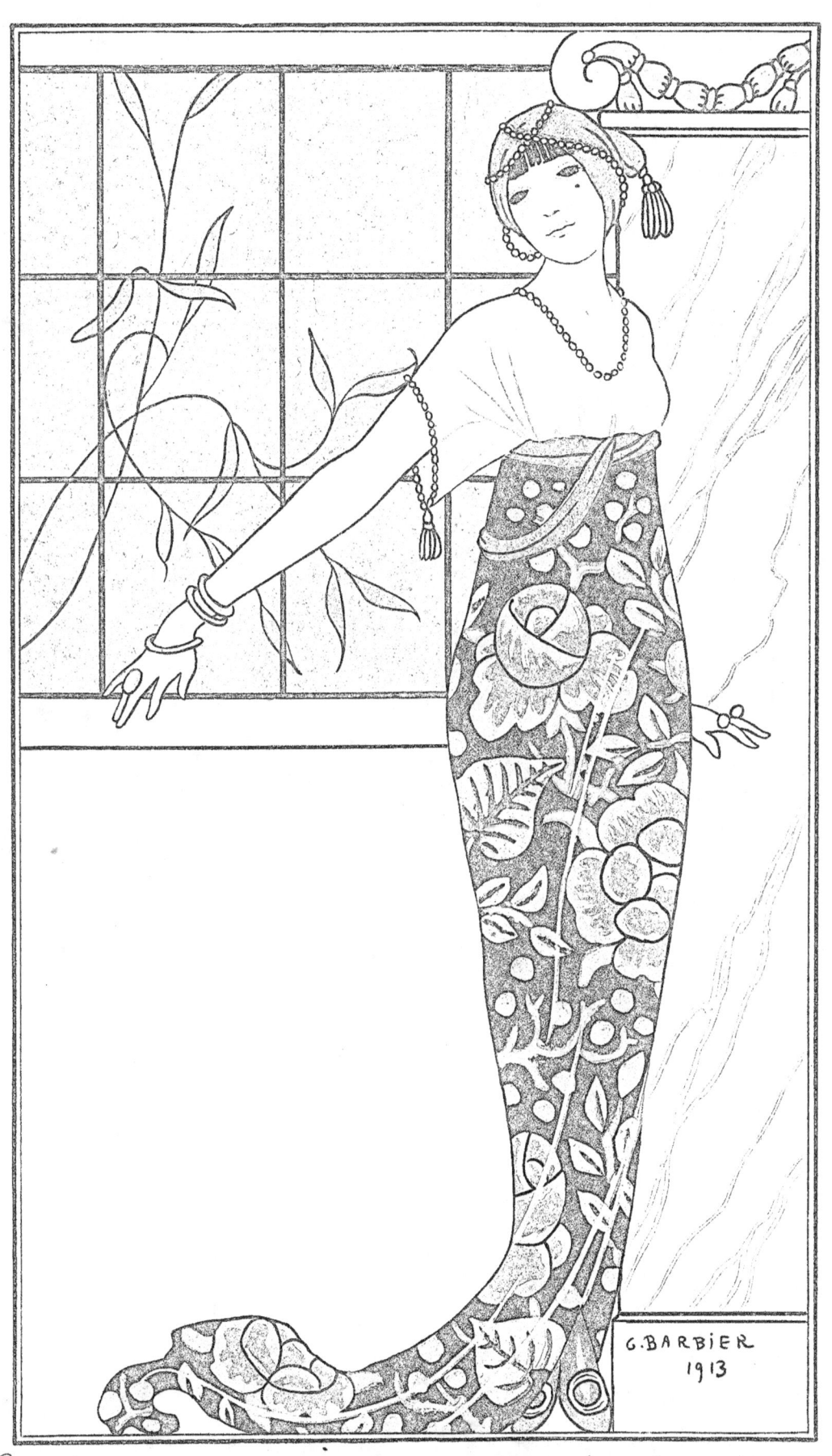

G. BARBIER
1913

Grande robe du soir, corsage de mousseline chair, tunique de soie
brodée dans le goût de la "Compagnie des Indes".

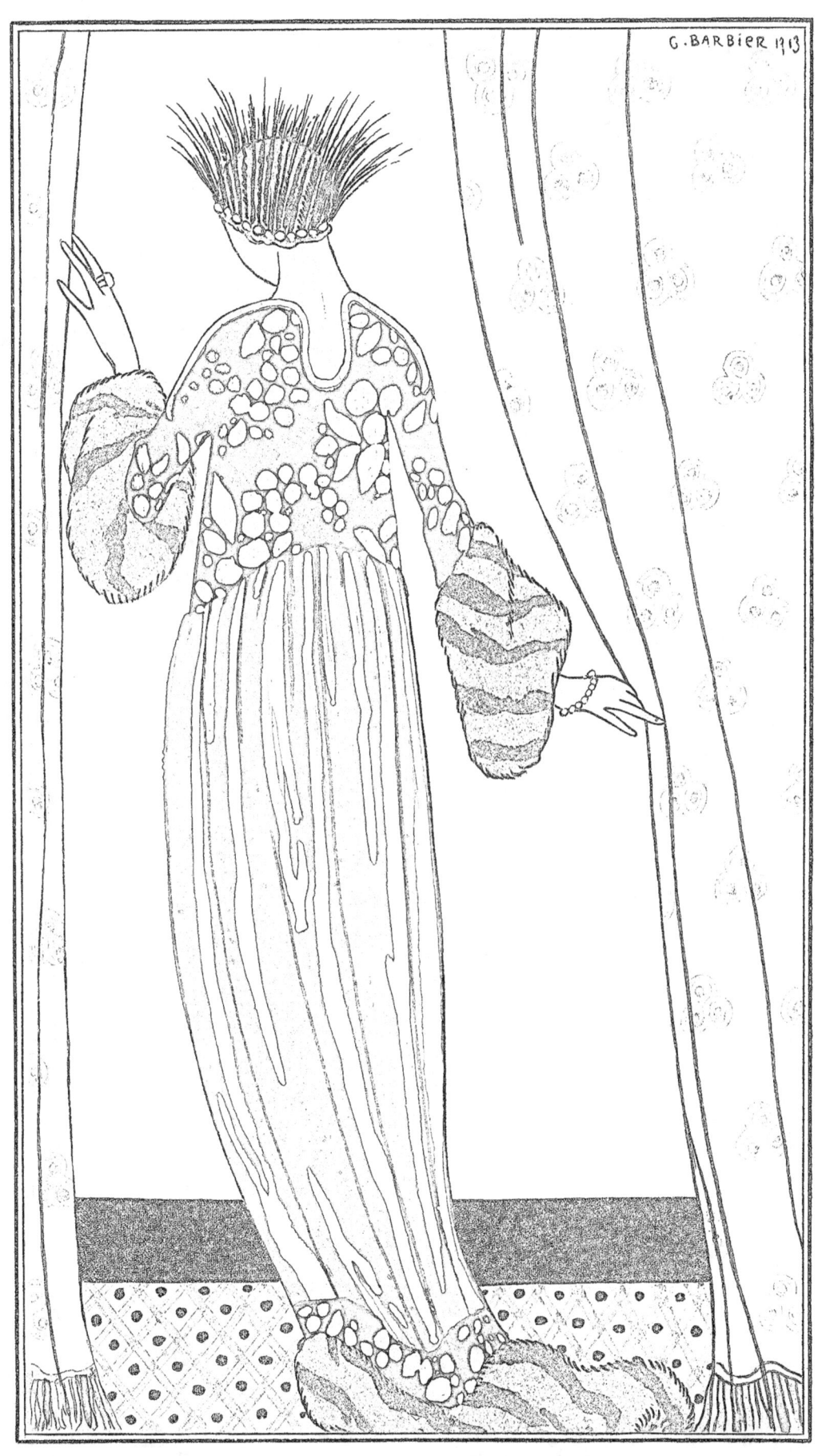

Manteau de Théâtre

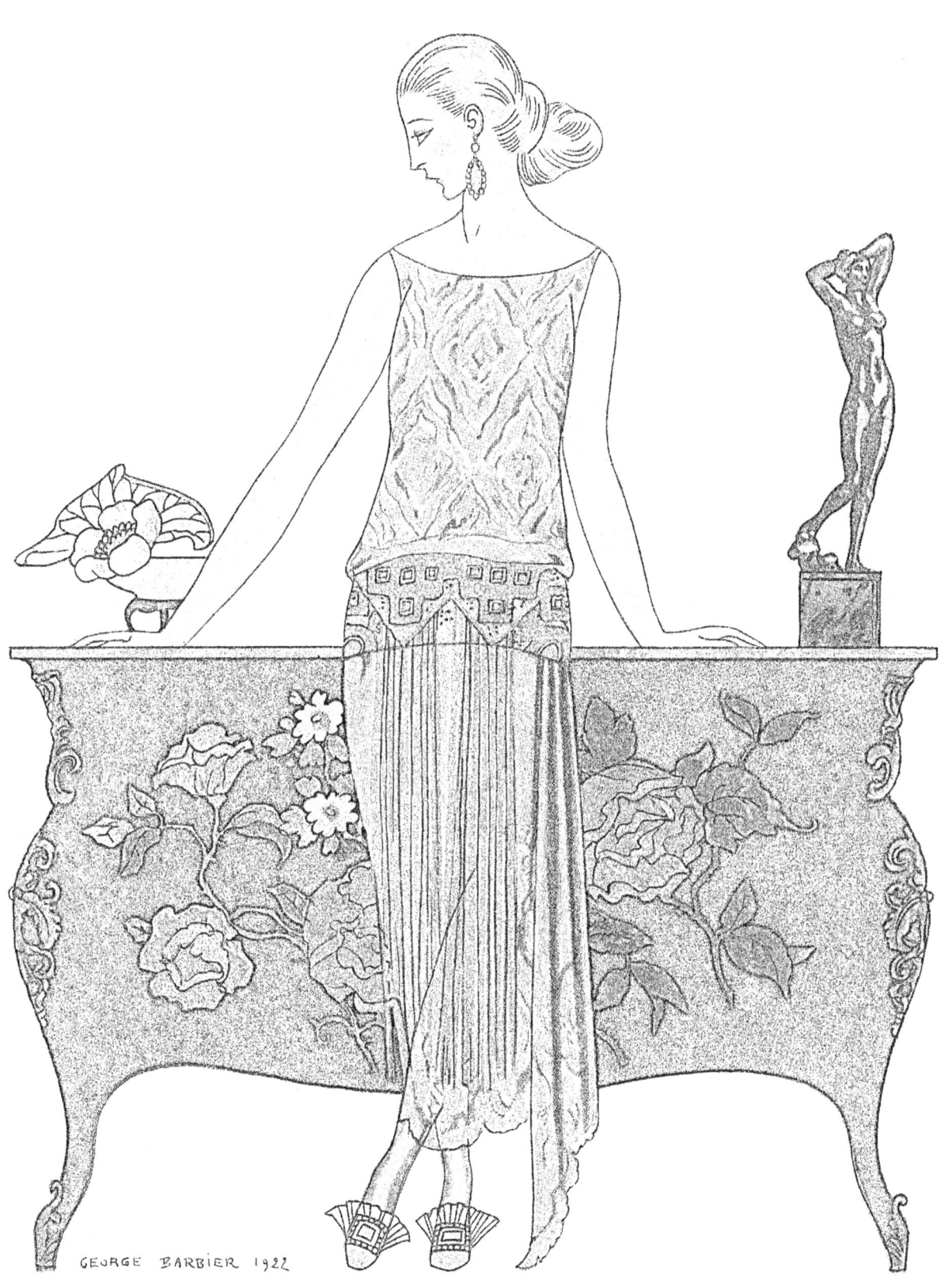

ROSALINDE

ROBE DU SOIR, DE WORTH

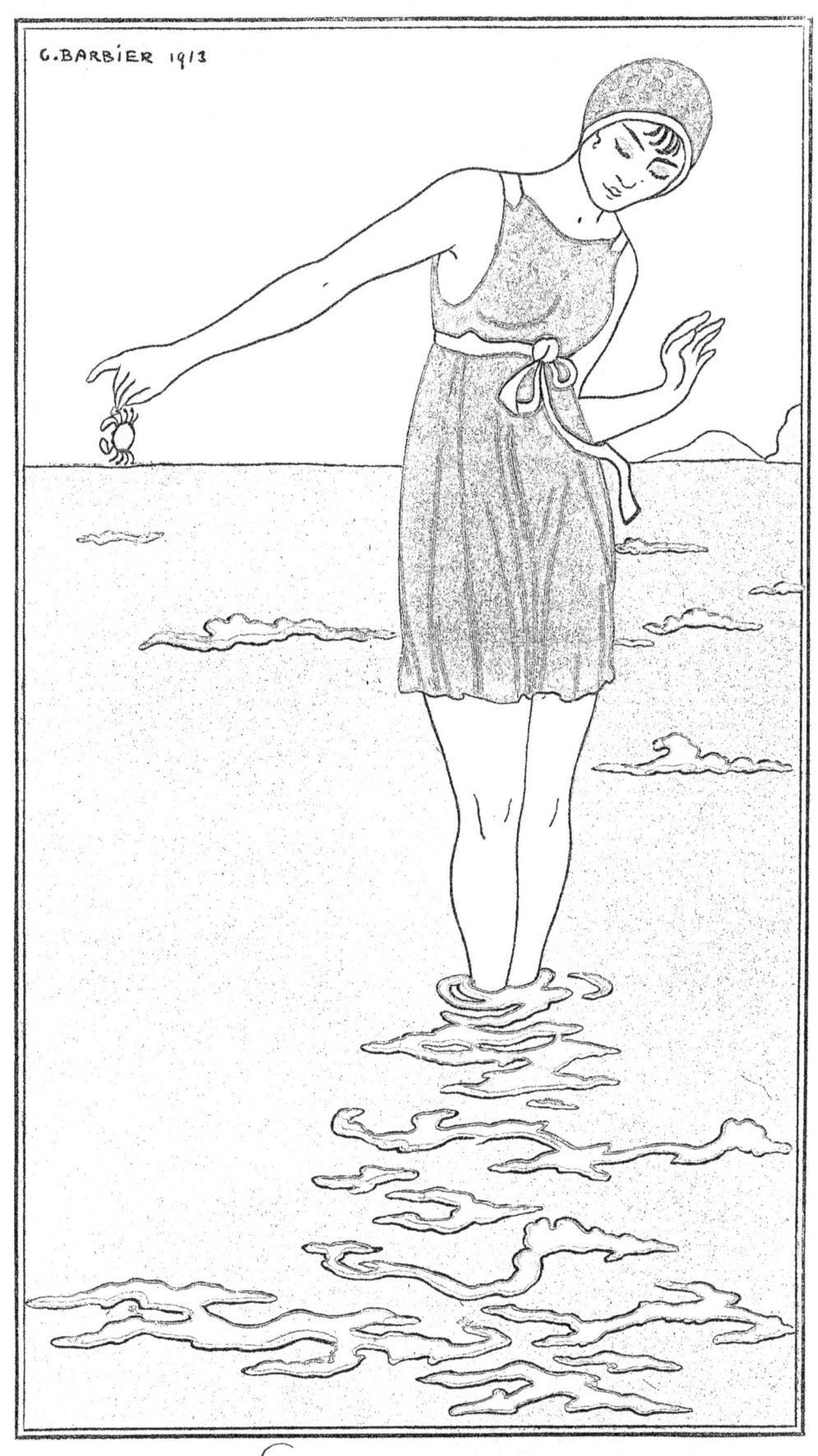

Costume de bain

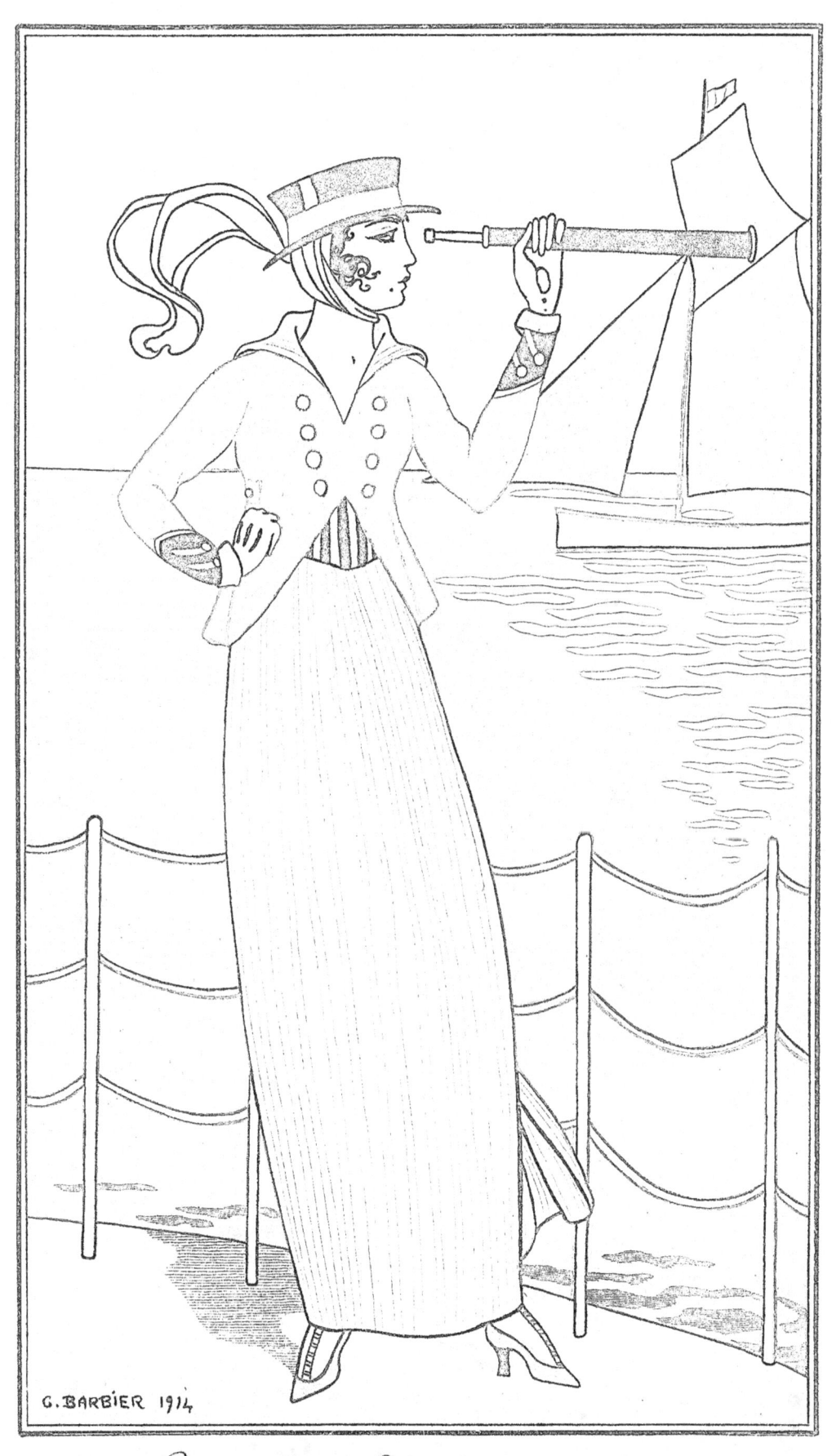

G. BARBIER 1914

Costume de Yacht: veste de drap,
jupe de toile, chapeau de cuir.

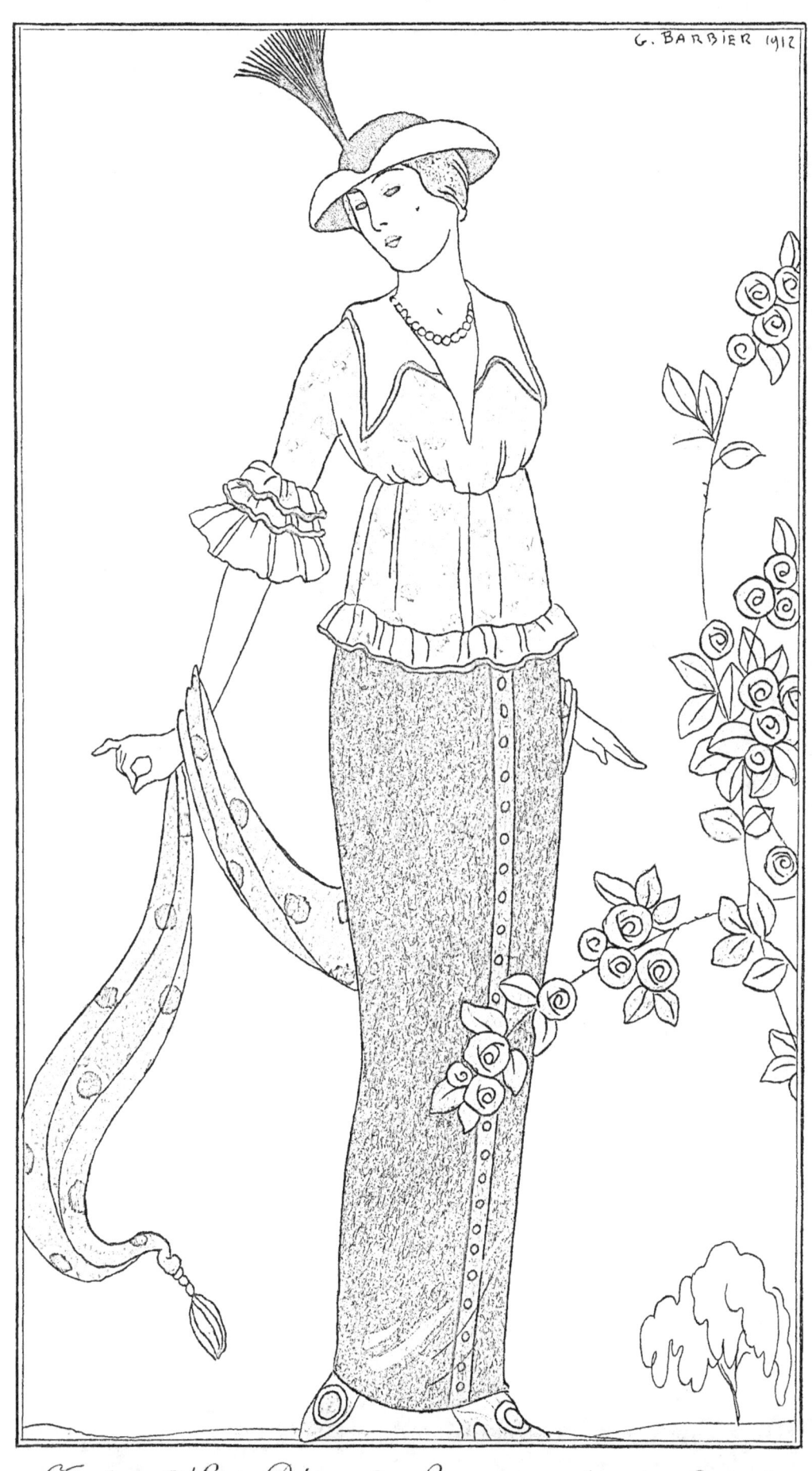

Toilette d'Été Blouse de Linon sur Jupe de foulard

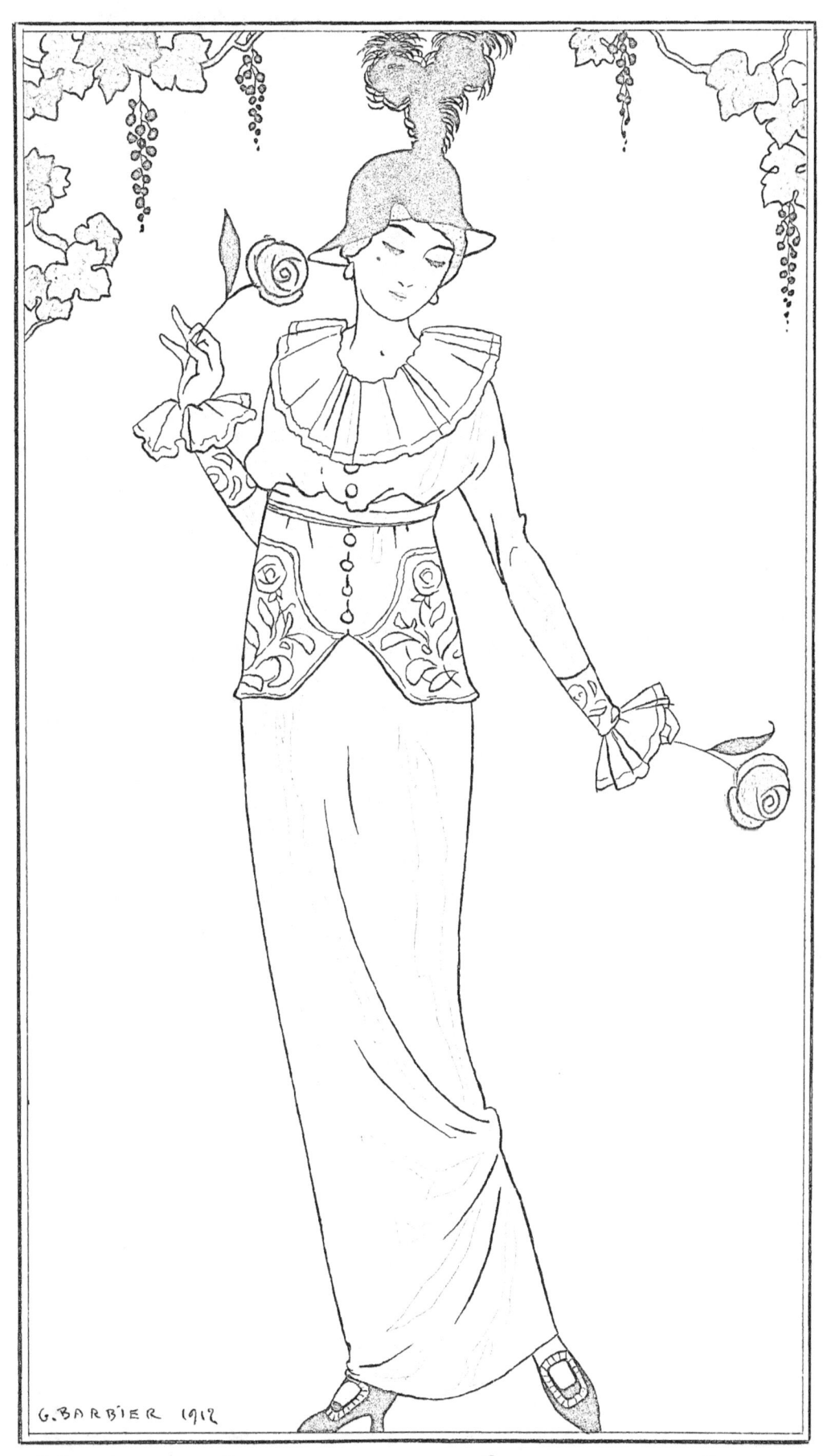

G. BARBIER 1912

Tailleur de Satin gris de perle, Chapeau de paille noir

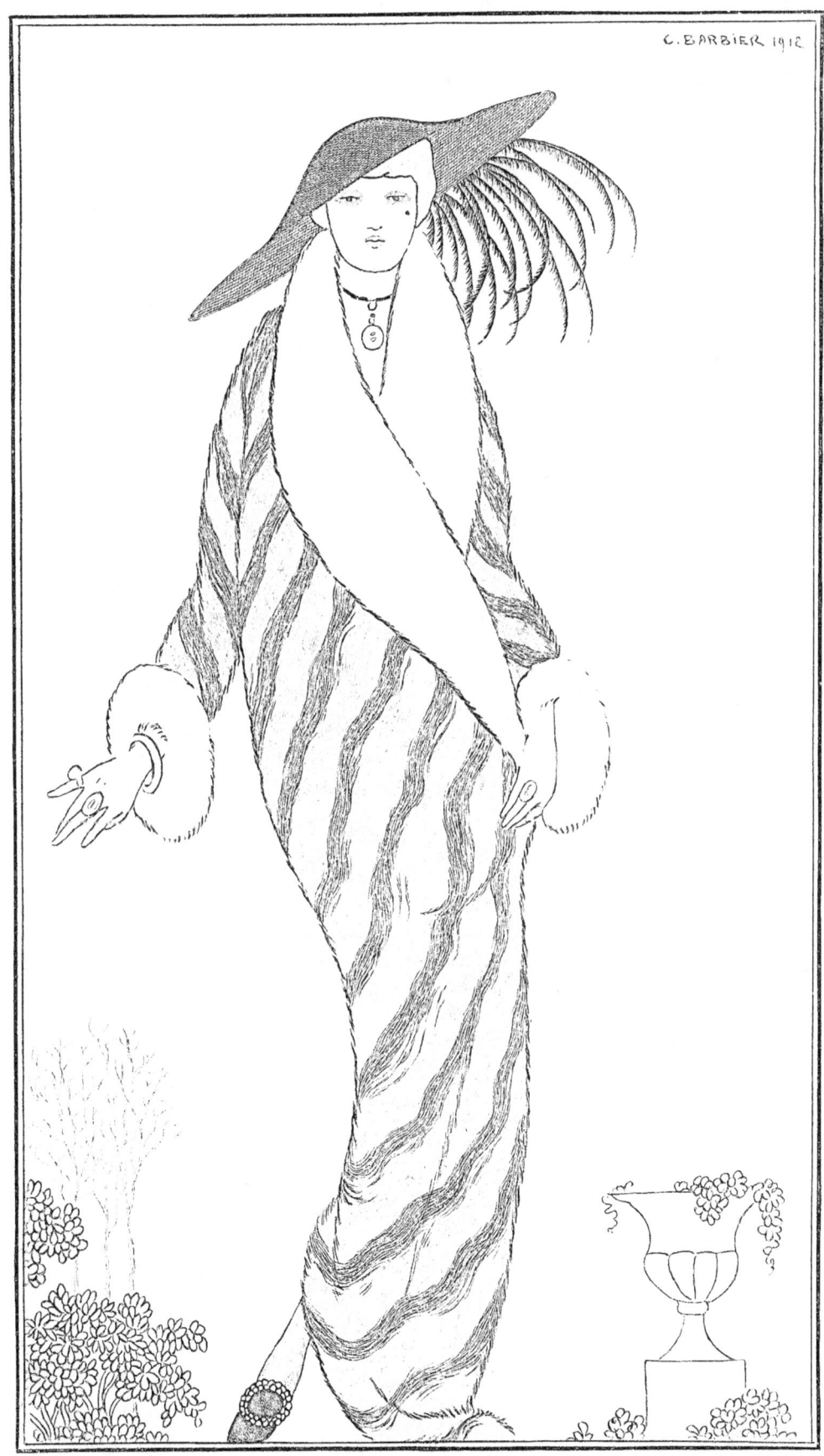

C.BARBIER 1912

Manteau de Zibeline à col et poignets de renard blanc

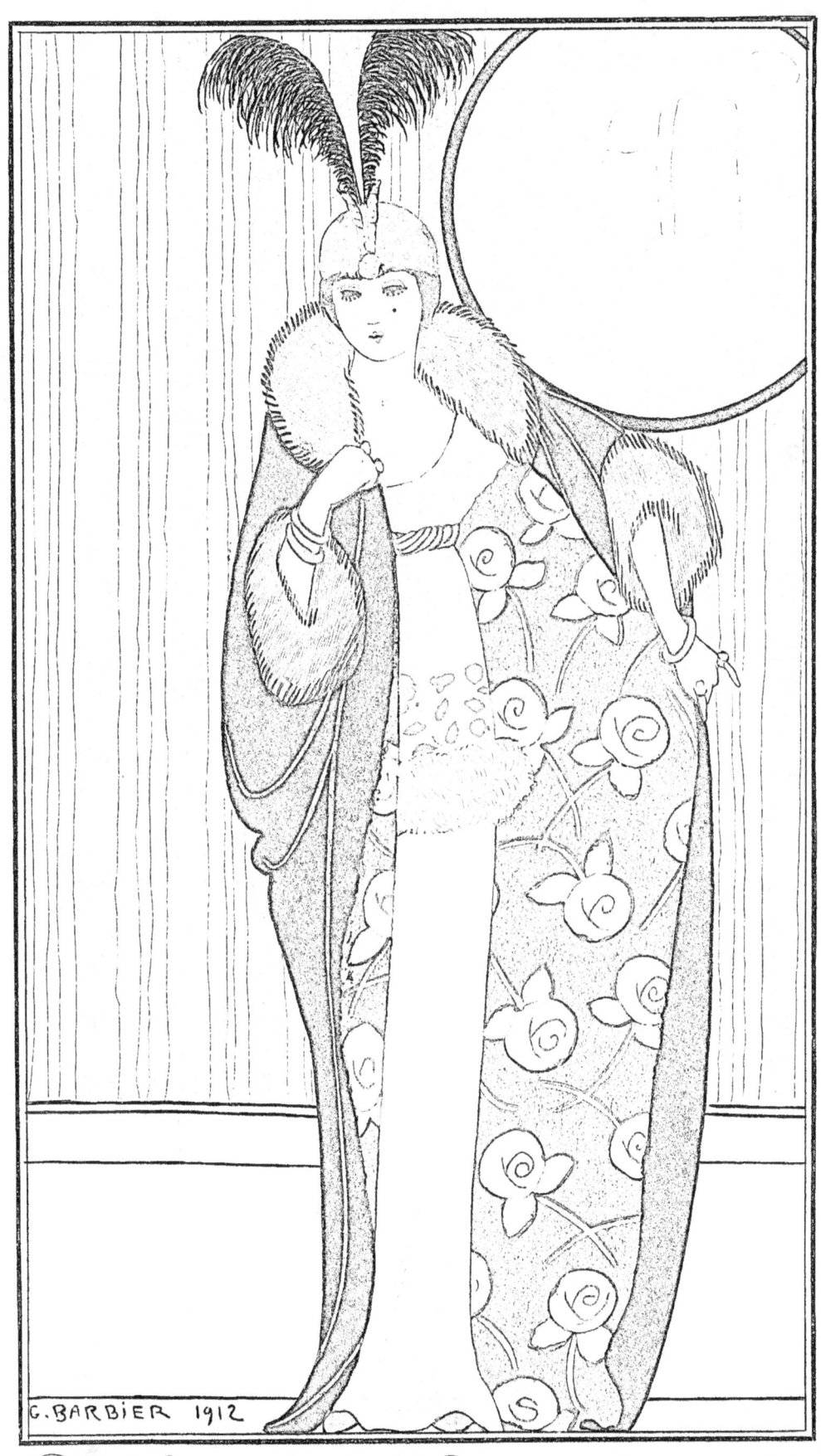

Robe de crêpe de Chine blanc garnie de renard
Manteau de loutre et skunks.

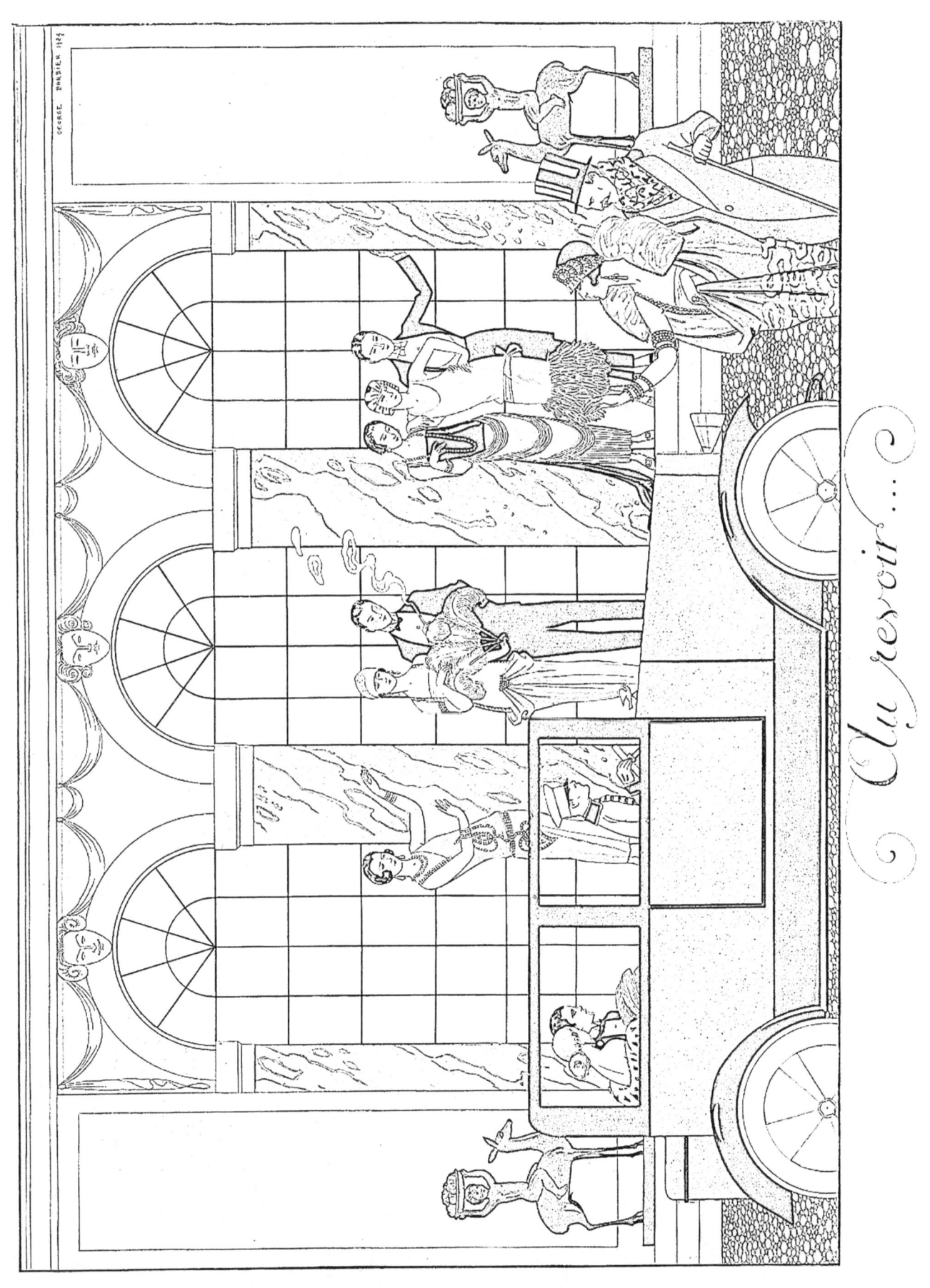